Today's African Woman!

Human Rights Champion and Single Mother

Suzanne Jambo
Mandela Ubuntu 2017 Laureate

ISBN-13: 978-0-9876141-9-3

All rights reserved. No part of this publication may be reproduced, stored in a retrieval system, or transmitted, in any form, or by any means, electronic, mechanical, photocopying, recording or otherwise, without the prior permission of the publishers.

This book is sold subject to the conditions that it shall not, by way of trade or otherwise, be lent, re-sold, hired out or otherwise circulated without the publisher's prior consent in any form of binding or cover other than in which it is published and without a similar condition including the condition being imposed on the subsequent purchaser.

Africa World Books Pty. Ltd.

Editors, Nathan Ellis (USA), Larry Ellis (Australia)

© 2018 Suzanne Jambo

This book is dedicated to all the children born into war.

Table of Contents

Background	7
Khartoum	11
United Kingdom	20
Kenya	24
Founding NESI	29
Introducing Motherhood	42
Dr John Garang	56
SPLM The Garang Years	62
Return to Khartoum	84
The Salva Kiir Years	88
The SPLM	125
The Diaspora	138
Africa's Brain Drain	142
Children of Freedom Fighters	146
Working With the Like Minded	151
Age, Gender, and Colour	155
Parenting	162
Final Thoughts	169
20 Questions for My Son	172
Photos	187

Background

The South Sudan civil war was a very complex one, and deeply rooted. Black African Sudanese were historically taken as slaves by Northern Arab Sudanese to Arabia (mainly Saudi Arabia and Kuwait) in the 1800s and early 1900s. Slavery in the region dates back much further. A shameful, most violating practice that did not catch the world's attention until the era of African colonization.

Sudan was colonized by the Ottoman Empire, with a result of tragically further entrenching the slave trade. The word Sudan (Aswad) means 'black' in Arabic.

According to British explorer (and abolitionist) Samuel Baker, who visited Khartoum in 1862, six decades after the British had declared the slave trade illegal in the Empire, it was the industry that kept Khartoum going as a bustling town.

Baker described the practice of raiding African villages to the south by slavers in Khartoum:

> An armed group would sail up the Nile, find a convenient African village, surround it during night and attack just before

dawn, burning huts and shooting. Women and young adults would be captured and bound with "forked poles on their shoulders", hands tied to the pole in front. Children were bound to their mothers. In order to render the village so poor that surviving inhabitants would be forced to collaborate with slavers on their next excursion against neighbouring villages, it would be looted of cattle, grain and ivory. Everything else was destroyed.

Historian Douglas H. Johnson also observed that by the late 19th century, two-thirds of Khartoum's population were slaves.

Then, the British ended up colonizing Sudan.

Like many Africans, I strongly stand against historical colonialism of Africa. However, a unique thing happened in Sudan. The British colonialists abolished slavery and entered into a condominium rule in 1899. This was known as 'Anglo-Egyptian rule'.

The British were more concerned about the Suez Canal as a strategic route to India and left Egypt to almost single-handedly rule Sudan.

The South was completely neglected, save for some missionaries that established churches and basic schools. This remained until Sudan gained its independence fully from Anglo-Egyptian rule on January 1, 1956. It was considered by Southerners as simply handing power over to the Northern Sudanese. Southerners would be subjects of the North.

The British focused on modernizing the north and left the south under the 'Closed Door Ordinance'. The claim was that the South was not ready for modernization.

BACKGROUND

By the 1950s, Northern Sudan was exploiting South Sudan's production of crops and animals by exporting such goods to Arabia. North Sudan basically used South Sudan as both cheap labour and "milked the cow", leaving it completely undeveloped.

Prior to this major event, in 1947, some prominent South Sudanese met in Juba. This was known as the "Juba Conference". They concluded that both the British Colonialists and their Egyptian counterparts would hand power over to the now empowered and groomed Northern Sudanese. That would thereby marginalize Southern Sudan and outlying communities such as the Nuba and Funj people of the Southern Blue Nile region.

The Juba Conference delegates determined that the south should begin to empower itself and be free. They began organizing themselves as a liberation movement. Anya Nya One was formed in 1955 in Torit, Eastern Equatoria, South Sudan. They demanded total independence from the north.

Of course, North Sudan would not hear this!

This led to the Anya Nya One war that lasted for 17 years. Tragic, with a dear loss of nearly one million innocent souls (mainly South Sudanese). A multitude was displaced.

Ethiopia, the only African country not colonized, took it upon itself to "save" South Sudan from the bloodshed.

Emperor Haile Selassie Mariam brokered a peace, and temporarily halted hostilities. Many influential South Sudanese conceded to this agreement for the sake of stopping the war. However, they knew too well that it fell far short of independence from the North.

Upon the discovery of oil in the 1980s, Sudan's President Jaafar Numeiri signed agreements with the American oil company Chevron to explore and drill for oil. The level of exploitation and discrimination towards the South increased dramatically.

The flow of blood increased with each barrel of oil discovered.

KHARTOUM

I grew up in Khartoum, in what was known as Sudan back then. Our humble neighbourhood Al Deim was in quite an old cosmopolitan area in the northern part of the city. I became very familiar with it.

My family and our loving mother Mrs Margaret Samson Jambo were everything to me. My mom was strong, focused, and determined in how she raised us. Ours was a family that protected itself from any harm, perceived or otherwise.

We were equally divided in gender. My two older sisters, Jackeline and my late sister Mary, did not grow up with us. They lived with their father since their early years.

I was born as a lone child to my, by then, single mother. I was followed by three brothers: Daniel, Emmanuel, and Anan Jambo. My early childhood days were mostly spent with them. I was always with my brothers to the extent that I played soccer in the neighbourhood with them, and it was accepted.

You see girls were not allowed 'culturally' to play soccer with boys, but I did. All thanks to my brothers who had my back. However, with the escalating enforcement of Islamic laws, I was forced to quit playing with them when I was about seven.

I learned everything from hovering around my aunts and uncles. They were frequent visitors to our home. Our mother absolutely loved to host her family. They talked about politics and our history nonstop.

At about 10 years old, all the political talk, the issues of social justice and marginalization, began to really sink in. Those family conversations taught me a lot. "What could I do?" or "Who should I be, so I can help?" was often on my mind.

We were surrounded by Northern (Arab/Islamic) Sudanese. They were friendly and kind in many ways. However, we were perceived as being different.

The undeniable fact that we were black, Southern Sudanese and Christians, did not work in our favour. We had the same tastes in almost everything, including music, food, and culture. We would show our humanity toward one another, but we always had a barrier between us. We celebrated their Islamic festivals of Eid Al Fitr and Eid Ramadhan. But they did not reciprocate regarding ours, such as Christmas. We recognized their Friday as being a national day off, but they did not acknowledge our Sunday. That being said, in the western world Sunday is recognized as the day of rest and they do not recognise Friday as such.

We went about our two parallel, yet conflicting lives until we left the country when I was fourteen. I loved the atmosphere, rhythmic lifestyle, culture, the food, and the smiles. Yes, a lot of smiles. I do remember my life in Khartoum well.

However, I did not like the segregation. It confused me. There were extremes in everything. I saw beautiful human feelings reach toward one another, but also a silent hate building. They hated us for being different. They hated us for wanting to be equal.

But they could also be nice people. How on earth could a child understand that? I was terribly torn inside. Never at peace, or happy.

Growing up in Khartoum was tough. It was further religiously polarized upon the declaration of Sharia Laws in 1983. The powers were intent on denying the right of worship and other basic freedoms to millions of Christians. I could not understand why this was allowed.

Life began to change. Sharia Law was affecting the schools, our relationships with our neighbours, public transport, and countless other facets of life. Moslems had the upper hand everywhere. The rest of us had to simply adapt and try to fit in. There was no free socializing between the two groups. My life became increasingly limited to school, home and the church. Such was the scope of my days as a teenager in Khartoum.

The times I most enjoyed, was being with other South Sudanese. Luckily, we went to Comboni (Catholic) Sisters school. It was one of the most renowned schools in Sudan for the quality of its curriculum and discipline.

Our Mother also introduced us to the church, to which we went regularly (Sunday school and prayers). As well, the Catholic Church did regular interactive programs, such as afternoon Bible teaching classes for those who were ready to be confirmed in their faith.

Other cultural activities included church-sponsored picnics, grouped by age. There we would enjoy days together as Christians in Khartoum having fun. Such gatherings included non-Sudanese such as Coptic Egyptians, Greeks, Catholic Armenians, Christian Syrians, and Ethiopian refugees, amongst others.

I grew up in the 80s knowing and interacting with such families in Khartoum. I learned that they fled their countries due to religious and ethnic persecution, and settled in Sudan. They became closer to us than we were to the Islamic Sudanese. We bonded together without any political or civic consciousness. It was natural. We all went to similar schools and churches, so we were like one big Christian family.

I am sure it was the freedom to express ourselves when we were together, that strengthened our bond. A respite from the sneers and injuries to our faith. We felt very safe together in our own island of peace. It became a beautiful and unique blending of cultures with no persecution. Just being ourselves.

Yes, these were the moments I still recall vividly. Some of the best memories of my childhood in Khartoum. The times when we identified ourselves as one people without prejudice to our ethnicities and nationalities. Of being equal.

This peaceful feeling ran through us all. One loving group of people relaxing. I miss that a lot, as it shaped my knowledge of boundary-free love. Total harmony. No racism. True survival, and being understood without question.

Back then, how could a black South Sudanese totally feel good being friends with a white Greek, and vice versa? Yet, we were. However, we could not feel the same regarding our own fellow North Sudanese Muslim brethren.

These are genuine questions that an innocent like myself was always puzzled by.

However, the comforting and soothing memories I shall forever cherish. It exposed me to boundless love and became the embryo of my universality with the common good. It taught me that there is such a thing as a universal race. That there is universal love, and that circumstances can bind completely different people together when survival was the common goal.

Conversely, falsely manufactured prejudices divide people sharply. Needless to add, hatred from the Moslem Sudanese made me learn that discrimination was a socio-cultural part of day-to-day life. I often felt like the Arabs wished so hard to get into our minds, souls and even our colour, just to change us. To remove our identity from us by force, and to replace it with theirs.

It hurt, and deeply so. I probably rebelled in my soul at an early age due to my exposure to persecution. I instinctively wanted to defend myself from this inner-most invasion. Survival instinct indeed!

To this day I am the same. If there is anything I abhor vehemently, it is when I realize someone wants to shape my thinking in any form whatsoever. I would never do this to another person! I know how it feels. I would fight back endlessly against anyone trying to culturally or religiously assimilate others.

IT IS WRONG!

All this has shaped my outlook towards life. Yes, I am an advocate of promoting and accepting ourselves in all our beautiful diversity. Until humanity embraces this fully, we will continue to face prejudice and discrimination. You can kill the body, but you cannot kill the voice of: "I want to be myself!"

My early Khartoum childhood experiences hurt me deeply, and yet equally helped me awaken to be the person I am today. I also felt greatly empowered to a point beyond my own expectations.

I am a woman of firm beliefs and values. A woman who has the extreme inner strength and stamina to continuously advocate, champion, and love the issues of humanity.

I will not relent until I see smiles growing on the faces of others.

I feel their hurt deeply. I relate, connect, and aspire together with others so that their desires can be heard. We all must be empowered and work towards our own emancipation and happiness.

An incident happened that changed me drastically when I was 11 it was 1988. We were all watching prime news in Khartoum at around 9pm. Very important court proceedings were being televised about Moslem Sudanese leader Mahmoud Mohamed Taha. The crime he had committed was to advocate that Moslems and Christians live side by side peacefully, and equally, in Sudan.

In an increasingly Islam-centric state, the government wouldn't tolerate this type of advocacy. The President of Sudan, Jaafer Numeiri (1969-1991) abhorred this man's preaching. So, after a sham trial, he was sentenced to death.

On the eve of this sentence, we were all sitting breathlessly around our television set in utter disbelief. The camera person zoomed in the face of the Mahmoud Taha, and something spoke to my soul. It was more than my young mind could comprehend. I consciously decided I must become a champion of the oppressed and the voiceless. A human rights activist.

Regarding my daily life, I was mostly either in school, at St. Peter and Paul Catholic Church (mostly on Sundays), or at home. That was my routine.

KHARTOUM

When I turned eleven, I was elected to be the chair of the Youth League in the Church. As well I was an active member of the Legio Maria and was elected as the Parish Secretary at 14. There I sat next to old wise men, including our two Catholic priests, while they deliberated the Parish affairs and made decisions.

I was only the secretary, so I did not speak much unless it had something to do with youth affairs or Legio Maria.

Otherwise, my role was to take minutes and read out the summarized decisions from the monthly Parish meetings.

Meanwhile, in the predominantly Christian south, the revolt against the regime had escalated into war. Ironically, these events created a large influx of internally displaced persons (IDPs) into the north, Khartoum included. The Catholic Church, alongside others, stepped up their humanitarian support.

In the local church that I went to since I was a child, hundreds of IDPs were housed. I found myself, now aged 12, volunteering to assist in their feeding and general welfare. The same church decided to open a few other facilities on the outskirts of Khartoum where land was more available. Once again, I accompanied the Parish Priest, along with other volunteers, to assist the thousands of displaced persons. Our Church also decided to open an adult literacy centre. It was there for those who mainly were engaged in manual labour, such as construction.

I volunteered as a teacher of adult learners and struck up a special friendship with these people. It seems they admired the courage it took for me to teach those of a far greater age than myself. However, it also educated me when I sat down with them for hours and listened to their interesting, although rather painful stories. This hardened my determination to become a champion of the voiceless.

My young life was overly occupied and busy. Going to school, the church, varied activities, and home was a load. However, I was content and was contributing toward the betterment of people's lives. I felt an immense sense of fulfilment.

I am forever grateful for my Khartoum experience. It shaped my outlook on life internally and externally. It fostered my ability to identify with the inner hurt of my fellow beings. My aspiration has always been that they rise and join hands with their fellows. I continue to miss my childhood friends to this day. Many of them never knew tribalism and grew up naturally as people who freely interacted with one another. My foreign compatriots were similar too. They all are the mosaic binding a beautiful, peaceful, and most harmonious phase in my early life.

Often, I reminisce to this day about them with great fondness. Though I was very young, I could feel how amazing that experience was. The ideal world I would always wish to be living in today. In a sense, it was my summer of love. This experience instrumentally and significantly shaped who I am.

Sadly, one by one, those families all left Khartoum. After Sharia Law began, many Christians, whether of Sudanese origin or foreign, gradually began leaving the country.

Every school year from then onwards, I began losing friends. They never came back. Many simply left without saying goodbye. We were too young to understand final goodbyes anyway.

By the late 80s, I completely lost touch with all of them. That was a most painful experience for me. They were friends with whom I had shared school breaks, lunch, and snacks with. Those with whom I used to play sports, and those with whom I simply used to laugh and joke.

It felt empty and hollow inside. Suddenly the sense of being alone gripped many of us who were still in Khartoum. We felt more isolated by the day. At least I had my family.

The years went by, and I completed high school. A beautiful and fortunate family story happened. Our big sisters decided to come and live with us. We became a happy six kids. We were now all together with our Mother. Being reunited was one of my happiest childhood memories.

In addition, we had a change of plan in the family. Our Mother decided it was time to leave Khartoum, as it was increasingly becoming unbearable to live as a non-Moslem.

Though we were young, the decision did not surprise us.

Khartoum never felt like home, really. Our loyalty to it was muted and always has been. Bitter and sweet. Lovely and painful. Home and not home. We accepted Mama's decision and truly wanted to get out.

We could not go to South Sudan, as it was engulfed in war. We could not remain where we were either.

Mom even abandoned her pension, to which she was entitled after working with Sudan Telecommunications for 24 dedicated years. She gave away our furniture and left us with only a few clothes.

We temporarily moved to Cairo in 1992. I was about 16 years old and armed only with a high school certificate.

We did not have any means of income. Mother did not have a job awaiting her in Egypt. She took a leap into the unknown. Luckily, she had two cousins who had lived in Egypt for over 20 years. We had an offer to temporarily live with either of them. With many thanks, we accepted.

My dream was to return to South Sudan someday to champion our peoples rights. At least that part came true.

United Kingdom

My choice to study law was deeply embedded in my heart. From a young age, I have always wanted to be a champion for people's rights.

By the time I was in high school, I had enrolled myself in evening classes of photography. I thought thereby I could be a journalist in Khartoum and expose Bashir's dictatorial regime. I would ease the people's suffering. Writing for the media was the focus of my dreams. We didn t have social networks then. Newspapers, radio and television only. In the countryside, there was mostly only word of mouth.

But, by age 16 I changed my direction and made plans to study law. I did so, in order to influence civil rights and policy-makers on constitutional grounds.

The "flashpoint" incident that inspired me to gravitate towards the study of law was a searing one. It was the case of Mahmoud Mohamed Taha that I covered in the previous chapter. His death galvanized me.

An opportunity arose through the Church for me to visit Kenya in 1993. While there, I met a most wonderful group of

Catholic church clergy. One stood out amongst the rest, and he treated me like his own daughter.

This was the late Italian Bishop, Caesar Mazzolari. He was working for South Sudanese churches in war-torn areas and had managed to establish about seven primary schools. Some of these were for girls.

The Bishop had a strong belief that we all had a right to an education. He worked with parents and local communities to further this goal. I was quite impressed and applied for a scholarship from his church to go and study law.

When I first approached him with my plan, I honestly did not think he would take me seriously. There I was, barely sixteen years old. Who thinks they should be allowed to travel to the United Kingdom to study law at that age!

To my surprise, his reply was, "Suzanne, you will make an eloquent and strong lawyer."

He agreed to further my request. Henceforth, after a seemingly very short wait, at seventeen I found myself on a London-bound flight to attend school at the University of Buckingham.

Due to my relatively young age, foreign schooling, and background, I had to undergo a thorough vetting. I found myself being interviewed by a panel of four Law professors. It was not easy, but I was determined and was successfully enrolled into the University.

While there, I was an avid student. My passion for human rights kept me awake many nights.

I was fortunate to link up with a group of British volunteers who had worked in Sudan. We decided to form a rights-based magazine called 'Sudan Update'.

We took paper clippings from all the news sources we

could find pertaining to human rights in Sudan. This became my Saturday volunteer job. It helped enrich and solidify my commitment to peace, human, and women's rights.

I learned a lot from Sudan Update, where I worked with ex-Sudan personnel such as Mr Peter Verney. This continued till I graduated from Buckingham University with a law degree (LLB) in 1997.

My minor fame also led to a voluntary role with Amnesty International at the London Secretariat – North Africa Desk. The North Africa Desk Officer, Dr Liz Hodgins, was very good to me.

I would help translate items from Arabic into English. This included some leaked human rights violations reports on Tunisia, Morocco, and Algeria.

The education received regarding campaigns, and the articulation of petitions was invaluable. The gathering of information, and how to keep the public alert on critical human rights violations around the Globe was very fulfilling. This enriched my outlook and my commitment.

I was married in a very literal sense to my activism and saw an opportunity in every situation to further human rights and/or promote peace. I slept, ate, and drank ideas on how to achieve these lofty goals. Since the age of 14 little else had ever crossed my mind.

The sole purpose of my university studies was to ensure I would contribute to constitutions, policies, and practices that were just. Others of my age had dreams too, but they mostly tended to live a more balanced lifestyle. They laughed, joked, partied, and dressed up trendily. Basically, they lived as normal young adults should.

UNITED KINGDOM

I did not! Parties, social gatherings, and general, light-hearted activities were to be avoided. My passion for social justice was all-consuming. In a sense that is not entirely unusual. Strong emotions are to be expected at that age. Mine have simply never left.

My four years there were fulfilling and passed quickly. It was now time to go back to Africa!

Kenya

My professional career began at age twenty-three, as a young female armed with a Bachelor of Laws degree. I was fanatic about the history of South Sudan and its 40 years of struggle for equality, justice, and freedom.

After a brief stay in the USA, where my mother and other family members were given refuge, I knew it was time to return to Africa. Back to London I went.

From there I obtained a one-way flight to Nairobi. A journey to the unknown! There was neither family or friends in Kenya.

Once settled, the United Nations was my first entry point. It was the world's premier global humanitarian and human rights body. I had the background qualifications and volunteer experience from university. It was worth a shot.

I was fortunate to get brief employment with the UN World Food Programme. I had a most wonderful boss, Ms Brenda Barton. A committed professional, from whom I learned a lot regarding public relations and media work.

The UN had a massive consortium of over 40 international NGOs, plus UNICEF, and a UN WFP called Operation Lifeline

Sudan, OLS, in Kenya. This was my entry point to contribute to help save South Sudan.

Humanitarian intervention by 1997 was desperately needed. As many as one thousand South Sudanese were dying daily from famine.

My contract ended, and I quickly found another temporary job with OLS. There, I worked with another great boss, Mr Hamish Young. He oriented me regarding the different factions found in the war zone. I had to be politically neutral and professional in my work as a humanitarian principles officer.

That's exactly where I thought I would fit in best. With my law background and my passion for human rights, it was a perfect fit.

This entailed training regarding humanitarian principles (the Geneva Protocols) and UN human rights conventions (such as the Rights of the Child (CRC)), and the Convention on the Elimination of all Forms of Discrimination Against Women (CEDAW).

Beautiful and noble!

However, my audience was not "easy". I had to train military commanders, traditional communities, and elders on women's and children's rights. Things such as not allowing youths to join the army below the age of 18. For girls not to be married below that age as well.

These were taboos in traditional South Sudan then. My passion for human rights blinded me to think that everyone would embrace these concepts to the degree I did.

Unless you were a victim, no one cared. Even then, few did.

After all, the traditions and customs for centuries allowed young girls to be married when virtually children. In addition, after 40 years of civil conflicts, the culture of violence became the norm.

Regularly, under-aged boys joined the army. Raping women and girls was an accepted practice. It was not easy at all to explain the Geneva Protocols, CRC and CEDAW in an environment of total lawlessness.

The region had been embroiled in civil conflicts since 1955. The culture of militarization and chauvinism were very challenging to address for a female. I sat for days with women in the hope that they may see how important it was for them to become agents of change. To understand that they need to defend their daughters from being married too young. To ensure that their boys did not join the guerrilla army below the legal age of 18.

I used my love and passion for justice, human rights, my love for children, and my love for the great people of South Sudan. They are those who have been oppressed for centuries, and who are my people. I belonged to them.

Initially, very little progress was to be made. Fortunately, the Sudan People's Liberation Movement (SPLM) was the main champion of the cause for justice, equality, and liberty for the South Sudanese people. They had entered into a binding agreement with UNICEF in 1997 called the 'Ground Rules'.

This document encompassed the Convention on the Rights of the Child (CRC). I used it as my Bible to assist in reasoning with military commanders and community leaders. Since the SPLM was highly revered by the people, we would make some progress.

I was privileged to be one of the implementers and travelled extensively all over the warzones controlled by armed rebels. I was on a mission to "save" children and women. Some of the places I had to travel were very near to the front lines. Gunfire was a constant companion. It was traumatic, but I was on a quest.

KENYA

With this commitment, I tried my best to always remind SPLM commanders that they were obligated to implement the Ground Rules Agreement. Amazingly, they listened!

Many children were spared from being forced into the SPLM army. As well, UNICEF and the Save the Children Fund, did their best to work closely with local authorities of the SPLM to encourage schooling and provide incentives for girls to join schools.

This also worked well. I made sure I spent endless hours with mothers, sharing my own personal experience regarding the importance of education for girls.

Gradually, and with aid from SPLM broadcasts on equality between men and women, we were making some progress.

The optimist in me was rekindled. I felt extremely fulfilled that, albeit, in small ways, we were able to save many boys from forced military conscription, and underage girls from forced early marriages.

We ushered in a new generation of girls' and boys' rights.

We were able to help many traditionalist South Sudanese to begin to question whether some of those traditions were not all that perfect.

As well, many began thinking their children deserved to go to schools instead of being in the army or getting married. No matter how small our success was, South Sudan was never the same when it came to girls' and boys' rights.

There was something missing in my work, however. My burning desire was to reach the grassroots population as one of them, not as an expatriate.

I began to get very active in human rights conferences and meetings. This included participating in Kenya's first constitutional drafting series of workshops in the late 1990s. Then there were several meetings on the Great Lakes peace-building blocks (DRC, Rwanda & Burundi). That was quite a volatile region at the time.

During my brief, one-year tenure with UNICEF, I felt immensely fulfilled. I also learned a lot, especially regarding theories on human rights. As noble and useful as they are, every country has its context. It all depends on our level of individual understanding, abilities, and connectivity with the local people. Rigidity, ego, and bullying are certainly the wrong approach. Simplicity, being human, and patience is key.

Meanwhile, via South Sudan, I met many like-minded individuals, and we began a network of national NGOs named the New Sudanese Indigenous (NESI) Network.

It was to be the saviour of me in so many ways!!!

Founding NESI

As a note: There will be references in this chapter to working with Dr Garang as many of these events 'dovetailed' together. I have covered those events in the chapter specifically dedicated to him.

By 1995 there were many international NGOs and two main UN giants: UN World Food Programme (WFP), and UNICEF. All these organizations coordinated their work in Sudan under the entity of Operation Lifeline Sudan or OLS. It was a huge consortium with a budget of more than one hundred and fifty million US dollars, per year.

Monies were spent on humanitarian, emergency, and very basic social services such as make-shift clinics, basic primary schools and adult education.

The UN-WFP was by far the largest in terms of humanitarian assistance. OLS also saved countless lives.

Southern Sudan had two types of wars: Mini intra-conflicts (militia groups fighting one another), and Micro wars between the Islamic Sudan Government of Bashir against the Sudan People's Liberation Movement. The SPLM was led by the late Dr John Garang on behalf of the oppressed people of Sudan.

South Sudan was also experiencing large-scale drought. The OLS created a major aid corridor and earnestly worked to swiftly save lives. This included air drops of food where UN-WFP relief planes could not land.

By 1997 it was reported there were about one thousand South Sudanese dying daily from famine. It was a real human tragedy on an epic scale. The vicious cycle of wars, relieved with bursts of humanitarian intervention, had been unrelenting since 1995. It seemed no one bothered to ask: "Why not stop the war!"

By 1999, a group of seven concerned South Sudanese and myself decided to come together, brainstorm, and bridge the gap. We wondered why hundreds of millions of dollars were pumped into South Sudan to save lives, yet the war continued unchecked.

Why not address the root causes of this disaster! These like-minded Sudanese were Dr Sitouna Abdalla Osman, Mrs Rebecca Nyandeng de Mabior (Dr John Garang's wife), Mr Lawrence Korbandy, the late Philip Neroun, Ms. Anisia Achieng and Dr Dau Alier, and myself.

We agreed that an indigenous civil society platform of national NGOs and activists could reach out to our isolated communities, hear their problems and their opinions regarding solutions.

As well, we could formulate the research and articulate messages to the world. This would include the warring parties. There was no civil society forum in war-torn South Sudan then. It was unheard of.

FOUNDING NESI

There were great challenges, resistance, and widespread mockery of our meagre work.

We sought partnership with NOVIB (Oxfam Netherlands). They saw the benefit and agreed to the plan in principle. The New Sudanese Indigenous NGOs were formed under the name: The NESI Network.

Noble ideas and visions started streaming in our heads. We felt that we could move mountains. Human rights became to us not only the physical violations but the right to exist as a human being. The right to basic social services such as personal security, food, health, and education. Yes, even the right to participate in the peace process.

It was officially launched in Nairobi, at the Silver Springs Hotel in March 2000. We had goals and ideals such as the restoration of a dignified lifestyle for the oppressed people of Sudan. For equality and justice, and a lasting peace. NESI took it upon itself to formulate the ideas and lobby them around the world. This would spread the rationalization that there is a direct link between man-made famine, wars, and humanitarian assistance.

Southern Sudanese were looked at as numbers to be fed by the international humanitarian community, while the SPLM looked at the South Sudanese as their subjects.

The SPLM felt they would be sufficient to represent them in the peace talks. The NESI Network membership was deeply marginalized. Local abilities were not recognized.

We began empowering ourselves. This started with articulating local context issues and situations, suggesting our solutions, consulting with local communities, and building consensus. We presented the issues in a manner that hopefully, both the

SPLM/IGAD and the international NGOs in South Sudan would understand.

It was no surprise I found myself "eating, breathing, and drinking" NESI ideals.

The world needed to shift its focus towards investing in peace. As the founder and coordinator of NESI, I worked around the clock to build consensus on these issues. I searched for ways to overcome our ethnic divides as South Sudanese.

By the 1990s, opinion was sharply polarized. We had to find common ground, and all see the bigger picture. We tried to reach out to all the parties.

NESI received hardly any attention. But we were not going to give up.

Fortunately, fate was on our side. I was invited to present a human rights discussion paper. It was hosted by the U.K. based Sudan Peace Group, in conjunction with the Ugandan-based Pana-African Movement. Off I went.

My colleagues and I worked tirelessly to champion for peace, human rights, and justice. I travelled the world and spoke passionately about the impending humanitarian catastrophe in South Sudan.

By 2001 there was a growing global movement of sympathizers, activists, and practitioners, advocating a just and lasting peace in Sudan. Conferences, groups, meetings, and petitions were organized worldwide.

The prospect of peace began looking up. NESI continued to educate the OLS consortium on the need to partner with national NGOs. Showing them how to provide sustainable quality services by, with, and for the people.

NOVIB (OXFAM NETHERLANDS), Norwegian People's Aid, NPA, Norwegian Church Aid, NCA, Pax Christi of

Netherlands, all started partnering with national NGOs. This was great. NESI was also able to shed light on a most critical matter. There was a direct link between famine and wars. Peace must be addressed.

In 1997 the government of Sudan granted rights to a consortium of oil companies including Sudan Petronas, PetroChina & Indonesia, Canadian-based Talisman, Netherlands Shell, and Swedish Lundin.

By 2000, a British based NGO (Christian Aid) was able to investigate regarding the direct link between oil activities in Sudan, and the killings of innocent South Sudanese.

They were able to author a report: "The Scorched Earth Policy". This proved that Bashir's government was responsible for forcibly depopulating indigenous peoples around the oil-bearing zones in South Sudan. All to pave way for oil exploration. This money allowed the north to purchase munitions and equipment used to kill South Sudanese. As well, they introduced policies of starvation by disallowing many humanitarian organizations to reach out to the internally displaced.

Christian Aid wrote widely on "Sudan's Blood Oil". Novib (Oxfam Netherlands) and Pax Christi also established a powerful group comprising over 20 international organizations under the European Consortium on Sudan Oil, ECOS.

NESI was the only South Sudanese national civil society invited. I was able, through NESI and ECOS facilitation, to address the EU Parliament in July 2002. By then the Dutch government was the rotational chair. As well, we informed the Dutch public via the media. News on Sudan oil fuelling the war sent ripples across Europe. This forced Lundin, Shell, and Talisman to pull out of Sudanese oil activities.

That left only the Sudanese government, the Chinese, and the Indonesians in the Sudan oil business.

None of those three countries governments are known for being notable humanitarians.

By 2002 the world knew that the Sudanese government under Bashir was a criminal enterprise which practised scorched earth policies, forced depopulation of indigenous people from their ancestral land, and purchased heavy arms to kill innocent South Sudanese.

Pressure began mounting on them to meaningfully open dialogue with the SPLM and sign a peace agreement.

NESI and other international organizations efforts started paying off. The political framework named The Machakos Protocol was signed in July 2002. It included strongly worded sections on human rights, women's rights, democracy, and civil society issues.

Later in that year, another landmark protocol was signed between the Sudan Government and the SPLM Cessation of Hostilities, CoH, November 2002.

This meant there would be no more attacks on civilians, by air or on the front lines. A breakthrough regarding NESI's message about the direct link between insecurity, war, and famine. People would now be able to cultivate and stay in their home areas to produce some food. Most of all, they would feel safer.

For once, the people need not fear the sky. Through aerial bombardment, Khartoum terrorized the people with constant air attacks.

NESI continued its campaign for peace. We never relented. We wrote petitions. We researched similar historical peace agreements. We prepared scenarios and shared them with the warring negotiating parties.

Gen. Lazarus Sumbiywu, the Kenyan chief mediator was extremely supportive of our work. He and I had a very good rapport. He genuinely wanted to mediate the talks until the peace was signed. He was committed. I admired that about him fully, and often shared NESI visions and ideas about peace with him.

From 2003 onwards, world representatives started migrating to Kenya to observe the progress in the peace process. They also met with the warring party's negotiators, including me.

Increasingly, I realized the world was interested in a lasting peace in Sudan. We had to ensure that the Horn and East African countries, realized the benefit of supporting a lasting agreement as well.

As NESI, we began organizing a series of public awareness, media interviews and peaceful demonstrations in East Africa, demanding a just and lasting peace for Sudan.

Then, a most historic event took place in Kenya: the UN Security Council decided to convene its Summit there. The first of its kind since its inception to be held on African soil. It took place in Nairobi, October 2004. It was resolved that a final peace agreement must be signed by December 31, 2004. This was amazing!

Sadly, Khartoum's Bashir government backed out and did not sign on the said date. It was the worst New Year's Eve. We cried all night, and our hopes for peace were shattered.

However, we didn't have to wait long. The big day finally arrived on January 9, 2005. Dignitaries arrived from Sudan, Africa, and around the Globe. They all came to witness the agreement that would end a war lasting almost 40 years.

You can imagine the HAPPINESS and ANTICIPATION.

No words can ever express it. You had to be present to have felt the atmosphere and seen the looks on people's faces.

There was electricity in the air, the streets, and even on buildings. I am not exaggerating. Nairobi was the crucible of peace!

A pre-interim period of 6-months was provided for in the CPA to draft an interim constitution and prepare for the formation of the two governments. They would be both in Khartoum and Juba.

Dr Garang appointed me and four others to draft it. Southern Sudan, as you can imagine, was a beehive of activity. We all thought that we were set, and ready for the peace agreement. We knew the framework. Drafting a constitution, however, was perhaps one major step that we overlooked.

NESI became my Plan B. Within months, we converged with other wonderful committed activists. We left our homes and worked tirelessly to produce a draft constitution.

Our 'office' was a Nairobi hotel. The Olive Garden, located in Kilimani.

We researched similar federal constitutions from around the world. By April 2005, our draft was ready. I printed out copies and met with the 'official' other four commissioners. We all agreed it was an excellent draft.

By May 2005, we delivered the documents.

All the while I was praying hard that none of the other commissioners would make any changes. They did not really participate in the draft due to work schedules, and the fast pace of events. There were provisions in the document that guaranteed human rights. We wanted it accepted as is.

My prayers were answered. We handed the first ever constitution for South Sudan over to Dr Garang, He, in turn,

FOUNDING NESI

handed it over to Sudan President Omar Bashir.

As per the agreement, Bashir had to assent to it immediately so Dr Garang could form his government in Southern Sudan by July.

All this while, NESI's seventy-seven separate member organizations worked on technically empowering themselves through capacity-building, organizational development.

They were also developing seven-year strategic multi-sectoral plans, and delivering basic social services to their respective communities.

We met regularly, held our monthly meetings, and formulated common action plans. All worked very smoothly and in solidarity. We were always reminded of the bigger picture: Southern Sudan, the Nuba Mountains, and Southern Blue Nile. In general, we represented all the oppressed people who must be free and equal.

As the coordinator, I presented discussion papers on NESI's behalf in numerous national, regional, and international forums.

This included:

The SIHA women's meeting in Djibouti on women's rights 2001, Botswana's Civil Society meeting 2003, South Africa's Human rights training 2003, Combating Violence in New York 2003, South Africa Xenophobia conference 2002, Sustainable Development conference 2002 Nairobi, Women in Leadership, Ghana 2008. Plus, Burma's technical need of my knowledge on how to form a civil society network during an armed conflict in Thailand 2009 and several other meetings.

There were many more conferences, meetings, and gatherings. All were regarding civil society and other works. NESI was my baby. It was my dream and the best platform for a civil society. It did not have barriers; ethnicity, age, gender, or ideology.

All we needed to do was to believe and be brave. To fight through advocacy, and lobby for a just, lasting peace for all. We would empower our communities. Men, women, young and old alike.

NESI was and still is, a unique civil society forum. It proved society can influence warring parties and the world. An organized, peaceful platform with a vision that can transform things in major ways. The impossible becomes possible!

Breaking Down Barriers
By 1999, the Intergovernmental Authority on Development peace facilitated talks had begun. Civil societies, women, and the youth were excluded.

We at NESI began championing for inclusion. As a result, I became the first and youngest female peace negotiator in IGAD. However, in a highly militarized atmosphere and an almost "exclusive" male club of negotiators, I found myself a lone ranger.

During the late 1990s, the talk of human rights, civil society, the participation of the voiceless in peacemaking processes, and political agreements was unheard of in the region. I tried my best to talk some sense into fellow peace negotiators.

I was told point blank: "You are a kid, a woman."

"What do you know about real wars?"

It stung and was a setback to my usefulness in participating in the process. With all due respect to IGAD, the neighbouring African countries' mediators (as well those in the international community & The International Partners Forum), they all didn't want to listen to a voice such as mine.

They had a tough enough time dealing with the warring parties. I had to make them listen!

FOUNDING NESI

I thought hard about how to forge a way to be able to influence them. I went back and forth to the NESI Network and worked closely with the East African media (particularly those in television). I made progress. I tried to garner public support in Kenya (the host country), along with the warring parties' negotiating teams and mediators. This tactic worked.

We wrote petitions with wide-ranging demands such as inclusivity, democracy, and human rights. I intermittently wore two hats, That of a peace negotiator, and of a civil society peace activist.

The representatives of African bodies of government, and the warring parties' negotiators did not make use of research for past similar cases back then.

Neither did they use computers. My civil society 'hat' was extremely useful. We were able to undertake research into several previous peace accords in other parts of the world.

We were also able to travel on fact-finding trips and documented them in writing. Mostly, this documentation evolved into NESI/civil society petitions and demands to the warring parties of Sudan. The civil society worked ahead of the negotiators and mediators. We surprised them often. I came in every day to participate in the peace talks, with both hard copies and floppy disks (there were no thumb drives or cloud storage in the late 1990s). Thusly armed, I was able to put forth stronger, more substantiated arguments than anyone else. This garnered respect from the older negotiators, as well as the mediators and the international community representatives. Our efforts had begun to pay off.

The subsequent years of the IGAD-facilitated Sudan peace talks broadened in scope, participation, and exposure. There was now inclusion of civil societies, human rights experts, and historians. It became the norm.

Furthermore, the talks spawned smaller working committees that travelled to Sudan and consulted with community groups. It was an admirable effort to investigate and record their wishes for a peaceful settlement to the conflict that had raged for such a long time.

Kenyan Chief Mediator, General Lazarus Sumbiywu, introduced many dynamic ideas. I personally believe they helped not only accelerate the peace process but also enabled in-depth understanding between the parties. There were so many underpinning issues that the world did not fully comprehend. He was equally

a tough mediator (being an army general), and a great listener. Conceptualized thought was his great asset. I also bombarded him with our NESI/civil society petitions.

In Conclusion

South Sudan from the late 1990s, through the opening decade of the new millennium, was almost a complete war zone. There were few roads if any.

Civilization was completely cut off from any form of any basic infrastructure and social services. It is a land naturally endowed with huge natural resources such as oil, water, land, organic produce, fisheries, animal husbandry, and gold.

However, due to systematic policies of discrimination and marginalization by Northern Sudan for centuries, South Sudan remained both illiterate, unskilled, and completely undeveloped. The NESI Network tried to do its part, with meagre support from external donors and partners. They took the risk to invest in empowering the formation of a society for civic betterment.

FOUNDING NESI

NESI was operating in an area where there was armed conflict. Not many donors by early 2000 could believe such a network could facilitate any change. To this day, I am personally grateful to both NOVIB and NPA for believing in NESI. It became "my constituency". In warring politics, no one listens to you if you are a mere civilian. You must be in the military or a high-flying UN representative. I had to work extremely hard, to ensure our voices might be heard. We were very successful in pushing forward our democratic and human rights agenda.

I will always be grateful to my colleagues in NESI:
Dr Sitona Osman
Ms Anisia Achieng,
Mama Rebecca Nayandeng de Mabior
Lawrence Korbandy,
Philip Neroun (RIP)
Dr Dau Alier
Mr Lazim Sulieman
Mr Gabriel Alaak

TOGETHER WE MADE IT POSSIBLE!!! Thank you to all my brothers and sisters in the NESI Network.

Introducing Motherhood

My life had become very full. As previously mentioned, I started my African career with UNICEF. I was a humanitarian principles officer. travelling all over Southern Sudan training communities and military commanders regarding children's and women's rights.

I met so many people. There were even military commanders who shared the vision of liberation, justice, equality, and freedom. I listened endlessly to girls, boys, mothers, and old folks relate their hopes and fears. Many spoke passionately about social justice, and I loved listening to that. In a sense, it made me overly optimistic that we could have an "ideal world".

About the time I helped form NESI, the dreams and visions really started flowing. I felt that we could empower ourselves as the first indigenous civil society aiding the marginalized areas of Sudan. I began to lobby for their rights.

Furthermore, we could enable these communities, and transform them where possible.

INTRODUCING MOTHERHOOD

It became a dream come true for me. I lived, breathed, and inhaled NESI.

We also networked with other like-minded civil society organizations within the East, Horn, and Southern Africa region.

During those years, to partner with a civil society group in an armed area such as Southern Sudan was unheard of. However, NESI was very persuasive.

We were genuinely concerned regarding the role we could positively play in the region. NESI interacted with local communities, heard their voices, and formulated these voices into convincing messages of peace, human rights, and civil society participation.

There was also the equally fortunate opportunity to have personally participated in countless human rights conferences, workshops, and discussions.

The travel was extensive. I managed to present discussion papers focussing on the "silent tragedy" of Southern Sudan. The violations including slavery, abductions, rape, marginalization policies, cultural assimilation, and forced Islamification. All this under the threat of aerial bombardment and helicopter gunship attacks.

The world cried with us once they heard the stories and saw pictures that we managed to present. As per usual, the media then reported, in an overly simplistic way, that the war in Sudan was only about Moslems versus Christians.

However, I tried my best to go beyond that. It was a political AND racial war. Islam was used by the North as a tool to gain support and sympathy from the Islamic world. This gave them a green light to kill as many Southern Sudanese and other marginalized dark-skinned Northern Sudanese as they wished.

It was ethnic cleansing, perpetrated so the North could gain full access to vast and rich Southern Sudanese resources.

That is why the SPLM began its war against these oppressive policies.

Meanwhile, as hard as it was for me to imagine, I also had a personal life! I met a seemingly wonderful man called Salah from the Nuba Mountains in 1999, and we began dating. He caught my eye (and mind) for his level of commitment to social justice issues. We married via a very low-key ceremony.

Within a year, I became pregnant.

At that time, I was in the middle of peace negotiations in Machakos (about an hour's drive from our rented home in Nairobi). There was a daily drive back and forth. Sitting for very long hours during these negotiations was normal. It was painful and exhausting both mentally and physically, but I insisted on continuing in the talks that often went on until past midnight.

I carried on till I was 8 months along in the pregnancy. All the while I was simultaneously coordinating the NESI Network advocacy work. Stacked on top of that was the media work to sustain the public and policymakers attention.

I simply could not afford to just lay down and relax.

But I so loved being pregnant. While driving long distances in traffic back and forth the peace talks, I talked to the baby in my womb.

The conversations with him/her (I refused to learn the gender) were about the work I was doing. Those were extremely calming, quality times. The baby was my private confidant.

Meanwhile, pregnant or not, I also had to travel frequently within the Region (East Africa) and into different parts of war-torn Southern Sudan. The travels went smoothly for the most part.

INTRODUCING MOTHERHOOD

However, we were once in Rumbek, Southern Sudan (July 2000) and there was a problem that needed our attention in the area. I was 5 months pregnant then and was there for consultations with the local community.

Upon take-off, while just gaining height, a Sudanese government Russian-made aerial Antonov started bombing Rumbek. One literally brushed one of our wings! The plane shook perilously, and the pilot decided to get us back on the ground.

We were all advised to deplane immediately upon landing and to run for cover in a bunker. Every airstrip in Southern Sudan had one for such instances.

Reaching it, I hit the ground without noticing what was in it. All I wanted was to cover my stomach from any attack. My baby's safety was my everything. Little did I know the bunker was filled with rainwater. It was also filled with snakes.

Stepping on them was preferable to the bombs falling from the sky though.

It all lasted seemingly forever. Then we were advised it was OK to come out. We had to rush back into the plane before the next attack.

We arrived safely in Lokichoggio, a border town between Kenya and Southern Sudan. From there, another flight took us to Nairobi.

This perhaps was the most thankful day of my life. I almost met death and I thought I might lose my baby.

However, there I was back safely in Nairobi, and we were both fine. I checked with my doctor the following day and all was well. I was so GRATEFUL!

The year 2000 continued with me juggling the IGAD Sudan peace negotiations throughout the region. My hours were filled with national, regional and international travels, advocacy, lobby work with the NESI Network, and other civil society activities.

I still managed to fully embrace my pregnancy. Like any other loving first-time, mom-to-be, I began gathering information. From my mother, aunties, and other experienced moms I became acquainted with the best motherhood practices.

They lovingly answered my numerous questions. I was truly getting excited by now and began preparing the baby cot. Shopping for a newborn! What a joy that was. Tiny beautiful stuff! I became elated with each passing day.

Then the first kick, on June 23, 2000. That's when I truly and fully realized what it all meant. AMAZING!

All the while, I was fully engaged in my multitude of public duties. No one knew how I felt inside. Ah well, the old guard treated me as per usual. Upon reflection, I suppose that's how they must have treated their wives when they were pregnant.

Peace talks are not a walk in the park! We generally discussed things calmly, but at times warring party negotiators brought in their fierce violent attitude to the negotiating table. Some arguments made good sense, while others were plain ego. A useless flexing of muscles. Reflections of the pure bitterness, and hostility that had been in them for a long time.

I do not blame them. Rather, I often felt sorry for them. Other times, I was incredibly angry. Perhaps my womanhood and youth looked at issues differently. One example was regarding the issue of power sharing. For me, it was all about the will to genuinely establish fairness. Once that is agreed upon, the sharing percentage would not make much of a difference. However, the opposing negotiators could not place values on issues such as fairness and justice.

INTRODUCING MOTHERHOOD

They saw this kind of outlook on issues as being "weak".

Semantics, terminologies and of course definitions were always far more important than the substance and intentions to them. Once I became empowered and recognized in the peace talks, I tried to intervene several times to remind the negotiators on such underpinning issues. The logic was that once we agree on intentions, a lot will fall into place. At times I was convincing, other times I failed miserably. They would almost hysterically laugh at me:

"She is so naive and meek."

It could be seen in their eyes. But once I stood back up to fight yet again, they began to see there was no choice but to work with me. I carried on and kept reminding myself that I was there for a purpose. My mission must be accomplished if there was to be any meaningful agreement. I would not let down my country, the civil society, the women's and human rights activists, and the voiceless masses. I had vowed to do so, and would do so!

Yes, my baby-to-be must be born into a better world!

I skipped the peace talks for two days prior to that. I had been getting super tired driving back and forth from Naivasha, where they had been relocated to. I was visiting my doctor weekly, and she advised me that I could deliver at any time.

Some of our brave, most wonderful, older South Sudanese women colleagues, with whom we worked together under the banner of SWAN (Sudanese Women in Nairobi), kept advising me to stop going to the peace talks. They could see my physical appearance was that of "imminent birth". It was something I could not comprehend fully as a first-time mother to be.

On the morning of December 6, I decided to drive to Biashara Street, Nairobi. It is well known for babies' necessities, and

I wanted to purchase a few more items. I also needed home groceries as I was not sure whether I would deliver normally, or through a caesarean cut. In the latter case, I would need to have bed rest for a lot longer.

In Sudanese culture, it was important to prepare a nutritious porridge as it helps with breastfeeding. By three in the afternoon, I had purchased all the necessary items and drove back home. However, by 5pm I felt severe cramps and increasing pain.

My Mother, who was with me at the time, had given birth to 6 children (including myself).

She was firm: "We need to go to the hospital. Your time has come Suzanne!" So, Mom and I drove there after she helped pack a few things. After a quick check, my doctor immediately wheeled me to the maternity wing. Yep, I was that ready to pop, and I was the last person to know!

Then began the serious labour pains. Fortunately, it lasted "only" about 10 hours.

I was reliably informed by all my kindly advisors that first childbirth labour pains could last 24-36 hours. Who knows, my constant overworking may have helped to reduce the length of my labour. I cannot truly ever know.

At 3am on December 7, 2000, my baby greeted the world!

My Mother and I had worked on finding an indigenous name for the baby; be it boy or girl. Names that had a "revolutionary/justice" type of meaning. So, we made up a new name. We combined two words: Dri (head), Tayi (Freedom) in Moru, a South Sudanese language (or Uhuru in Kiswahili). Put together it spells Dritayi.

Literally, Freedom of the Head.

INTRODUCING MOTHERHOOD

In a deeper sense, it means 'The ultimate freedom of any human being from any form of subjugation or restriction'. I added Tutu as a homage to South African Bishop Desmond Tutu, a man I always admired for his unwavering quest for peace.

My son's name became Dritayi Tutu. With the birth of my baby, my world changed.

I was now a mother, and many thoughts started racing through my head.

"How do I manage my overly busy public commitment, and care for my infant baby?"

I had no answers! I decided to go with the flow while fully prioritizing my baby over anything else.

Could I actually manage to do so? Time would tell.

When Dritayi was barely 10 days old, I absolutely had to attend a meeting. Both my Mother and a nanny filled the gap.

But the guilt I felt that day. Oh my god! I still feel it!

I left my unassuming, innocent, and most adorable creature, in their care.

However, there was no focusing on the meeting. No matter how hard I tried, my mind was with my son.

I kept reminding myself that there were millions of babies in Southern Sudan whose lives were at stake. There were thousands of pregnant women in Southern Sudan whose lives were at stake.

In the end, that was what kept me going.

When it was over, I raced home to my baby and held him like it was for the first and the last time. I cried so hard! It was the most painful moment for me as a new mother. I vowed that subsequent meetings and travels would be after my baby was more than 3 months old. If anyone desperately wanted to meet me, it had to be in my house and near my baby.

That worked miraculously well. The months went by, and both my son and I became 'strong' together.

I established a full office at home. In 2001 Kenya, that was not easy. I had a landline, internet, a desktop, some files, and a few other basics.

During the daytime, I gave my son my full attention. Playtime, breastfeeding, lots of hugs and kisses, diaper changing, and all manner of things. I napped when he napped. By 8 pm every night, he slept truly like the baby he is.

Now began my "me-time" (hot bath, some music and the computer). Then, back to the work at hand as an advocate for peace.

There were tons of emails to send and answer. I would work right through till about 3 am every night. That was generally when my son woke up for feeding or diaper changing. Often my colleagues and partners would see my emails and wondered how I worked such long hours.

Time passed and Dritayi was just over a year old. I had fully resumed my participation in the peace talks, running and managing the NESI Network, and continued to network and advocate on other peace issues.

I would seize on every given opportunity to drive back and spend even an hour with him. Do not ask me where I got the energy from. I juggled between all of that and few were aware that I had a one-year-old infant.

Then the travels began, and I did not enjoy that at all! I would only accept if the duration was less than a week. Anything longer, I rejected out of hand.

As I have mentioned before, NOVIB (Oxfam Netherlands) was one organization to which I am extremely indebted. They were NESI's main partner and part of the European Coalition Against Sudan Oil (ECOS).

They invited me to participate in its first Oil Conference in Brussels, during July 2002.

I could not decline such an opportunity! I accepted conditionally. On maternal grounds: I would come only if my baby could accompany me.

Pleasantly, super baby-friendly NOVIB (per Mr Gerard Steehouwer, the then Horn and East Africa programme manager) said a big yes. It was all facilitated. A baby-friendly hotel, a nanny, and flexible hours.

The duration of the trip was about two weeks. Meetings were held in both the Netherlands and Belgium. Plus, I was with my baby! A human rights/peace activist who is a new mother! Unthinkable for the South Sudanese. I was able to give it my all, and thankfully the three oil companies withdrew from Sudan. Thanks to NOVIB, ECOS, and to a small part, myself.

The months went by. My baby was growing in a loving and peaceful way. Perhaps it was from all the chats while driving that I had with him when he was still in my womb. Somehow, he was (and still is) an extremely supportive, peaceful, joyful, understanding, and accepting son.

I resumed my public duties fully, as there was a lot of movement in the peace negotiations. The world, and in particular the USA, began paying keen attention to the Sudan conflict. There was a major upswing in pressure. The regional and the international communities all wanted peace and began pushing the warring parties to accelerate the signing of an agreement.

From July 2002 onwards, a series of high-level world leaders visited to consult with us all (especially the Southern Sudanese) on what we wanted from such an agreement.

Parallel to the IGAD-facilitated Sudan Peace Talks in Kenya and starting late in 2001, the Southern Sudanese civil society (namely NESI Network and SWAN) held several peaceful rallies. Many Kenyans joined us. Wonderful Kenyan drivers parked their cars, paving way for us to walk on the streets with our peace placards.

NESI organized the youth, women, and Kenyan sympathizers to join these series of peaceful demonstrations for years. There were huge public and media attention. We wanted to add our own pressure to the UN's, other regional, and international entities, so peace would be accomplished.

During one of the demonstrations, I straddled my infant baby and we both demonstrated. He was less than one-year-old.

It was repeated regularly thereafter. Mother, son, and other activists demonstrating in the streets of Nairobi demanding that the peace agreement be signed. I remember a most moving moment when my son was barely 2 years old. He demanded to carry a placard. On it was written: "Give Peace a Chance". He insisted on standing and walking while holding the sign. Of course, heat, thirst, and fatigue took over quickly. After a few minutes, he asked me to carry him.

Whenever we were home together, it was our chance to catch up with each other.

Luckily, we were in a very good neighbourhood. That's another motherhood/parenting strategy that worked very well for us.

We had two siblings as our neighbours. One aged 3 years, and the other 7 months. Dritayi was 10 months old when they all met. They instantly bonded. We had a backyard small garden, and I kept it busy as a kid's playground. A swing, a sandpit, lots of water to make mud, a tree house, and of course safety and security measures for the kids.

They played endlessly while I worked away on my desktop.

I could easily see them in the garden playing and could hear their sweet baby voices. This was pure mental therapy and helped me to carry on working. My son would often come barging into my office, smile and run out. Knowing I was home made him feel super content. My happiness with the situation knew no bounds.

When Dritayi had reached two and a half years, it was time for him to begin school. Another tough step for every parent is when you realize that your child must go and join the real world without you.

I searched around for nearby kindergartens. Ones where my son would feel happy and safe.

My final choice rested on St. Christopher's Preparatory School. It was near our home, and it was a very cool 22-year old facility.

The first day I dropped my son at his new school (after days of talking him into it) was a challenge. He did not want to leave his 'Mummy'.

There were many kids in the classroom happily playing with each other. But my son clung to me, totally refusing to join them. I had to sit there for almost two hours as he gradually started familiarizing himself with the other kids. However, when I rose up to leave, he stopped everything and ran after me crying that he did not want to stay. He wanted to come with me!

Ms Christine Mwangi and Ms Jesse, two of the most wonderful nursery teachers, saved the day. Having vast experience with children, they knew how to comfort my boy until he let go.

I walked away feeling completely hollow and strange. I made sure I was out of my baby's sight, then leaned against a wall as I cried alone. The nauseating feeling in my stomach was caused by the huge sense of separation between us.

That's when I knew there was a change forever from the baby that I carried in my womb for nine months. The one that suckled my breasts and held me tightly like we would never, ever let go. Now, we were 'separated'.

That my friends is truly the way of life!

Days, months, and years passed by. I was back again in full swing pursuing my life of activism. Simultaneously, I continued to grow into the role of being a most loving mother to a most wonderful son. The first trip instance where I had to leave Kenya without him, Dritayi was aged four.

It was another most painful experience. He fell ill, having come down with a nasty flu and fever. Here I was, thousands of miles away and feeling hopeless. Then, this type of sickness seemed to repeat in some form every time I was travelling. The two beautiful teachers knew my son's mood would swing whenever

I travelled. They gave him extra love and attention, as did his nanny Lydia. She was a God-sent angel who gave her whole to my son, especially when I was away.

As time went by Dritayi began to distinguish and adjust to my times at home with him, and those when I had to travel. He immensely appreciated our times together.

His positive attitude taught me gratitude. He lived for the times we were together. Young as he was, he always assured me that he was fine. He even stopped getting sick.

His all-around performance in kindergarten was outstanding

in learning skills, social interaction, and sports. He excelled. All his school reports would reflect his good nature, and his ability to grasp ideas quickly and exceptionally well.

When he returned home each day, he joined his neighbourhood pals. By then they were truly like brother and sister to him, and inseparable. I also made sure, whenever I could, that he travelled with me.

I would write to the school requesting that he accompany me. They fully understood and would give him sufficient homework to keep him abreast of the other children.

He would dutifully complete his tasks while on these trips.

Dritayi turned five. He was now ready for grade one of primary school. Luckily, I was in Nairobi to witness his graduation. My best friend Amanda Majiso, and my photographer brother Emmanuel Jambo were also there with me.

That was a most wonderful day. MEMORABLE! My son and I proved to ourselves we could manage our unique circumstances, and overcome the challenges of my public life. He too became a true sympathizer of the cause and a joy to his mother!

Dr John Garang

I met Dr Garang (the late founder and leader of the Sudan People's Liberation Movement and Army, SPLM/A) in March 1998, during my participation at a Pan-African Movement facilitated-conference in Kampala, Uganda. There I made several interventions during the sessions. I was vocal, and justifiably so. It was a hall full of passionate human rights activists from all over Sudan, Sudanese Diaspora, and regional activists.

I saw him as a man with a huge presence. Confident, well-spoken, and could express himself clearly regarding almost any topic. He did so with flair and utmost confidence. A sharp spotter of talent, I must add. Although he did not attend the said conference, he was aware of it and had asked if several of us could meet him.

A group of us, about ten women participants, decided to go and meet the man. Safety in numbers! He met courteously with us and listened to the different points raised by the delegates. I did not speak. I listened. I was a new entrant to it all.

Thereafter, I returned to Girgiri, Nairobi. While seated at my desk in UNICEF's Operation Lifeline Sudan (OLS) offices, my extension rang. I was informed that I had visitors. There were none on my schedule for the day.

Curious, I walked out to the little garden where we staff normally sat. Who do I see? Dr John Garang in the flesh! My blood rushed all over my body and my head froze! The heavily bearded rebel leader, accompanied by his guards, was looking straight at me. He rose up, extended his hand, and asked whether there was a private place we could talk. I directed him over to the main UN cafeteria where we were able to find a decently quiet place.

Without any preamble, he said, "You belong with the SPLM!"

Once again, I felt the blood rush through my veins. My heart was beating through my chest! I felt honoured to serve such a just people's cause but equally afraid of entering a point of no return.

I could not reply to him right then. He seemed not to expect me to. The meeting was over.

The SPLM was a very formidable movement. However, like any other civilian (albeit, an activist), I had strong reservations regarding armed rebellion. I still do! I had to think!

I had sleepless nights. No one from my family would ever agree to such a thing.

Later, after sorting it all out in my mind, I found myself readily agreeing with him.

Subconsciously, I really wanted to join the struggle for our people's freedom. So, I did.

Fortunately, Dr John Garang had sensed in me charisma, and a passion for social justice and human rights. A passion combined with the commitment to do whatever necessary to achieve our goals.

There was no office desk or a space to work from. One just joins the SPLM and waits for assignments.

A couple of months passed, and Dr Garang issued an executive order appointing me as an advisor to the first SPLM Women's Conference. I was to draw up a draft regarding women's participation in policy, and the decision-making processes of the SPLM/A. This marked my official entrance into the movement and the start of more frequent meetings with Dr Garang.

Who, in a real sense, was this man?
I cannot exactly say that I knew him well. We never discussed anything beyond certain narrow topics. However, I listened closely and watched his speeches live from the sidelines. I learned so very much! He spoke vividly regarding a wide range of issues with clarity and intelligence. He could rationally have a discourse regarding anything. Women's rights, youth, democracy, the return to civilian rule, and his vision of "new" Sudan. All these subjects rolled easily off his tongue.

What was his speaking style?
He would speak in a measured way, non-stop. Often for no less than 2 hours at any given conference or gathering. I loved these talks because he gave an answer to almost every question. Included in those were the ones lingering in our mind that we otherwise would be too unsure to ask aloud.

He made things sound possible. He was resolute, very certain, and confident. If you are one burdened with a massive ego, self-centred, and possess a doubting type of personality, you might vehemently hate him.

If you had an uncertain, timid and less-confident personality, Dr Garang picked you up and boosted you to new heights.

If you were visionary and action-oriented, you would love him.

His style of presenting solutions won you over completely, and you would have very little to argue with him about.

I mean, I seriously wanted us to achieve justice, peace, and move toward a better destiny. Dr Garang was the leader I wanted to work with.

However, he was not perfect. I did hear of his leaning toward tribalism and favouritism. Again, I was too young to understand such practices in detail then.

I cannot for certain say this against him. It was my personal perception at the time. I know for certain that Dr Garang was always moving forward towards better solutions.

Sadly, some 'parties' personal ambitions and misconceptions, may have sometimes gotten in the way. This may have led perhaps to some extremely damaging levels of conflict. So much so, that some ended up as foes of Dr Garang and set them in direct opposition to him.

The dynamics of wars of liberation often are a factor in artfully delaying certain democratic elements and pillars of justice.

As well, the enemy and external friends alike, were hard to manage. Internal issues continuously demanded attention. But Dr Garang was a truly visionary leader. Of that, I have no doubt. A smart strategist. Sharp as a tack, and a prodigious reader.

Often, we travelled for months at a time. During such trips, I got closer to him. He had a fourteen hour plus workday, and I was there. During meetings, I sat and listened endlessly to him explain our struggle eloquently to all. I could see how mesmerized the audiences were.

Western world representatives from places such as Norway, Finland, Denmark, and Sweden would pose questions. Dr Garang patiently and convincingly answered them all.

He never missed an opportunity to push our collective agenda and was a believer in cadres that could competently supplement his words. Often, we would be in high profile meetings. He would pause and abruptly ask me to supplement points he was making. This always took me off guard, however, it showed how he believed in a young inexperienced person whom he knew was committed and visionary. One who could effectively augment the proceedings. This boosted my firm belief in him and did the same to my self-confidence. These experiences also really exposed me to the western world.

What do I think of him?
Sometime around 2003, I approached D. Garang to ask for a meeting. He agreed. I told him the women I spoke with were asking why it was the PhD holders (referring to Dr Garang, Dr Riek Machar, and Dr Lam Akol) who were the ones disagreeing to an extreme level, and prolonging our war.

Dr Garang looked me in the eye and said: "I promise to deliver a just, lasting peace."

That wasn't the PhD talking, it was the man himself. I understood there and then that education had nothing to do with commitment to peace. A degree is in so many ways, just a piece of paper.

Anyone with the ability to retain information can get one. A person's 'word' and the keeping of it is the true measure of character. It is impossible to completely sum up a person, but I will try my best.

Dr Garang was a shrewd leader whose focus was set. He knew what he was doing at all times. He was a strategist, and was able to overcome endless challenges. Many of these were of an internal, in-fighting nature. There were many attempts to eliminate him.

Through it all, he focused on the bigger picture. Perhaps sometimes at the expense of details. These details later became serious governing issues regarding democracy within the SPLM.

However, he was able to unite all his forces and forge forward toward achieving a very detailed and extremely useful comprehensive peace agreement in 2005. He may have not been perfect, but he possessed great vision and the ability to 'walk the talk'.

At the end of the day, I still have mixed feelings. I suppose we could say the same if we were being honest about any great leader. They are unforgettable, flawed, and unique.

SPLM THE GARANG YEARS

The Sudan People's Liberation Movement was incepted in 1983 by the late Dr John Garang, with critical help from others.

In September of that year, President Numeiri proclaimed "Al Sharia Al Islamiya Limaza!" (Why we need Islamic Sharia Law!).

This phrase became his "everyday" refrain, prior to imposing Sharia Law on all Sudanese.

Dr Garang was by then a colonel in the Sudanese national army. Like many educated South Sudanese (especially as a former Any Nya One young officer), he realized the country was headed towards greater Arab-Islamic domination.

This was a clear abrogation of the 1972 Addis Ababa peace agreement.

Khartoum was bent on a systematic policy of exploiting every natural resource found in South Sudan. Those funds were used to purchase arms to kill those in the South.

Numeiri's declaration not only provoked the South Sudanese but also opened up old wounds. Many were forced to tolerate second-class citizenry, discrimination, and exploitation.

SPLM THE GARANG YEARS

By May 1983, the SPLM began its war for liberation, equality, and justice for all oppressed Sudanese. It based its operations in South Sudan, led by Garang and his colleagues. This time around, there was widespread media coverage from radio and television. The SPLM had its own radio station, and prime news time was at 3 pm. This was the hour after the standard end of the workday in the country.

I was about 9 years old when my Mother, along with her brothers and sisters, were all gathered around the radio. It was tuned in to the SPLM radio station. I would sit quietly on the floor, listening to both the broadcast and my family's comments.

I could see sparkles of hope in their eyes.

It was set to a low volume. In Khartoum, if you are found listening to the SPLM, immediate arrest followed. You were most likely never to be seen again by anyone. SPLM radio gave us all the news. How they organized themselves, where they are, and how many they were. They also had revolutionary songs to raise morale.

We felt, and as little as I was, I too felt that soon we would be free from Khartoum's oppression. When Dr Garang came on the radio and spoke, we listened to every word he said. He spoke strategically, eloquently, and raised our hopes higher and higher every time.

Khartoum on the other hand, in their media, did their best to call the SPLM rebels, outlaws, and murderers. Numeiri's government tried its best to tarnish the image of the SPLM and dismiss it. They also cracked down on many South Sudanese suspected to be SPLM sympathizers.

The political atmosphere in Khartoum was always tense. We South Sudanese kept to ourselves. We no longer socially mingled or interacted with Northern Sudanese for fear of any of them reporting us. Our parents cautioned us very strongly not to utter anything about the movement.

Being a rebel movement, the SPLM was rather restricted from officially interacting with African and world leaders. Dr Garang relied heavily on face to face connections. His trips to some countries had to be of the utmost secret. The SPLM was officially waging a war against the Republic of Sudan, a United

Nations member and an African Union member state. Neither body would want to be seen dealing with outlaws.

Garang was a very shrewd strategist. He knew all this and worked tirelessly to woo the trust and confidence of African leaders without exposing them. He was smoothly persuasive and was able to gain a great deal of sympathy as a result.

By the mid-1980s, former President Mugabe of Zimbabwe offered to become the host country for the SPLM main African office.

Then Ethiopia under President Mengistu Haile Mariam offered to host it. Much closer to home! However, in the 90s he was ousted by Meles Zenawai. The new Ethiopian prime minister expelled the SPLM from Ethiopia. They then moved the main African office to Nairobi, Kenya during President Daniel Arop Moi's tenure.

All these movements and relocations were both part of SPLM's efforts to protect foreign relations and to get logistical support. These strategic locations were crucial. So important in a world that hardly knew of the Southern Sudanese or their struggle.

Dr Garang moved frequently between the SPLM-liberated areas and African countries. He often met quietly with African leaders lobbying for South Sudan and the other marginalized communities in the country. His efforts created significant awareness and solidarity towards the cause.

During the mid-80s Ethiopia and Sudan famine, he facilitated and opened up corridors for international relief organizations into Southern Sudan. Thusly, the SPLM become the "recognized" local administrative authority in the region. It also made them more appealing to the world community. Continuing to act as a 'good broker' was of great benefit to the movement.

Gradually, these same organizations, in turn, began developing reports about Southern Sudan regarding humanitarian needs and human rights. Often these organizations were able to unearth violations both in SPLM-held areas and in Sudan government-controlled ones.

These same reports paved the way for the landmark signing of the Ground Rules Agreement with UNICEF. It marked the first time a UN body signed a convention with a rebel group. It laid out a framework for humanitarian and human rights conventions, binding on both the SPLM and the UN.

In summary, that is how SPLM foreign policy gradually developed. Their efforts at alliance and solidarity building paid off brilliantly. Sudan related issues began hitting the news internationally. Albeit, mostly on humanitarian grounds.

By 1998 the SPLM had liberated and controlled a large area of Southern Sudan. No one can possibly prepare you, regarding the dynamics of insiders when it comes to liberation movements. Guerrilla war tactics, systems, and hierarchy (where seniority complexes abound) are combined with old school attitudes and traditional pro-male views.

When Dr John Garang invited me (in early 1998) to join the Sudan People's Liberation Army, I was elated and completely frightened at the same time.

The SPLM army wing ruled all, and I was not army personnel. They fought real battles that I was not involved with. However, the excitement of belonging to a platform that based its principles on human rights and social justice overrode my fears. I dreamt of working with the like-minded to bring about justice for all the oppressed people of Sudan.

At the time, human rights and democracy were spoken of, but not actually practised in most of Africa. Dr Garang was a voracious reader. He had a proficient understanding of world dynamics, and how peoples in the developed world interacted with each other. He absorbed much from his time in America at Iowa State University. This perhaps explains how he embraced women's equality at a faster pace than his colleagues.

I joined the SPLM voluntarily and with optimism that my participation would make a change, however little it may be. No one warned me of the roadblocks and challenges that I would encounter.

In this chapter, I have provided the facts to the best of my recollection.

During June 1998, Dr Garang sent a note requesting my help to organize the first SPLM Women's Conference. The aim was to develop a policy regarding rights and equality for women and girls. I gave it my all. This was my golden opportunity to help alleviate the suffering of the most marginalized of the marginalized.

By August of that year, we were able to hold a conference in New Kush, South Sudan (SPLM HQ then).

The 700 delegates came from all over Southern Sudan, the Nuba Mountains, and Southern Blue Nile. They included traditional chiefs, elders, community leaders, and a good solid number of female representatives. The guest of honour was the then SPLM Vice Commander-in-chief, Commander Salva Kiir Mayardit (now the President of the Republic of South Sudan).

Dr Garang really wanted to be present at the conference. However, intelligence operatives alerted him and warned him not to go. Khartoum had plans in motion to target New Kush and assassinate him. He had to opt out, in order to save both his life and ours. Thankfully, the conference was not attacked.

As a speaker, I zeroed in on the negative implications and culture of militarized conflict.

We discussed how these have marginalized females; relegating them to less than human status.

The women and men who were present at the conference applauded. It was a unique platform in which to forward ideas that were radical to that particular audience.

This type of opportunity doesn't come easily or often. By God, I used it to the fullest. I drummed women's rights into their heads. The crowd clapped. Women, especially older women, openly shed tears. I felt their countless years of buried pain, silently endured. I cried and felt weak as a baby. It was an experience I have never encountered before. One I will never forget.

There was a sense of victory and justice in that hall. Unanimously the delegates adopted the "Resolutions of Equality for Women and Girls of Southern Sudan"!

Thereafter, I drafted the First SPLM 'Women's Policy and handed it over to Mama Keziah Lenywa, the then the SPLM Secretary for Gender and Child Welfare.

She approved it, and handed it over to the SPLM leaders where it was unanimously adopted.

This meant, via affirmative action principles, SPLM Policy enshrined that there would be a minimum of 25% women in all areas of public service. The balance of roles could be competed for by both sexes. Due to war and outdated traditions, women were oppressed in the region. The minimum percentage set aside for them as a means of redress.

To this day, it remains in effect. A significant hollow achievement. It languishes on paper unimplemented, despite numerous efforts by many to bring it into effect. The change must come from the mindset of the people, and of course the leadership and policymakers. The odds of that happening are slim to none.

As the years passed by, I continued to work closely with Dr Garang. He appointed me as a peace negotiator by the end of August 1998, when I was twenty-three. This made me the first female, and the youngest on the SPLM 10-member team working on the Intergovernmental Authority on Development (IGAD)-facilitated Sudan peace talks 1999-2005.

I travelled to Addis Ababa with him. There I met the great African/Kenyan politician-scholar, Professor Anyang Nyong'o, and South Sudanese leader Dr Lam Akol.

During this meeting, we discussed the need to resurrect peace negotiations in Kenya. Prior discussions were held in Abuja, Nigeria in the early 1990s. They did not yield much.

We returned and waited. By August 1999, IGAD began facilitating peace talks in Nairobi. Eventually, they were moved to Machakos and Naivasha, Kenya. I was virtually a full-time peace negotiator.

Earlier that year, in April, Dr Garang also formed a committee of 5 commissioners to review SPLM martial laws and to draft them into civil laws. He appointed me one of the five commissioners. Once more I found myself the only female and the youngest appointee.

In short order, we did our work and submitted it.

He was pleased, and orders were made to all Judges in SPLM controlled areas to implement the new civil laws. Handling dual roles was stressful. However, we were accomplishing things and it felt great.

The peace process was the most challenging task. Being a female, young, and having never carried a gun, I was an 'ornament' according to the old guards. They had fought in the wars since 1955. Most were resentful, angry, and extremely disrespectful toward me.

My participation raised some eyebrows throughout the SPLM hierarchy. "What will Suzanne Jambo, who is too young and a female, bring to a tableful of warriors!"

Negativity started, developed, and then escalated to abrasive levels. At times I was not allowed to sit in on some sessions or utter a word during others.

I would be told: "You are not required here!"

However, whenever Dr Garang was present, this totally changed. Everyone suddenly "respected" me, and accorded me a chance to contribute. They even applauded my input. During tea break times, some would approach me and exchange pleasantries. They complimented me on my fresh dynamic ideas, and how much they valued my contributions.

Hypocrites!

The libertarian politics of justice and equality were not embraced by most. I began noting the lip service and double standards I encountered. Imagine this happening in a movement that bases itself on liberating the oppressed? How depressing!

Many a time, I felt like quitting. But who would represent the issues if I left! I was under immense pressure, and I was not a quitter! I decided to go back to the drawing board. Back to Dr Garang, who appointed me as a delegate on his dysfunctional negotiating team.

He did not seem to want to hear me out. He felt there was no room for error. Fortunately, I had a plan B. I demanded the inclusion of issues such as human rights, women's and youth rights, democracy, the participation of the voiceless, civil society and good governance.

Dr Garang appreciated and understood the scope of the plan immediately. Our entire delegation was ordered to introduce these important concepts into the official SPLM position.

You see, by the late 1990s, such ideas were not important to many African governments; or liberation movements for that matter. Due to my success to date, I was able to book regular one-on-one meetings with him covering inclusive, progressive, and dynamic initiatives.

Every time, without fail, these became the SPLM's position at the negotiating table. I was the only 'authority' on the subject they had apparently. The regional and world communities began looking at the SPLM as a viable 'progressive' liberation movement.

Media world-wide began reporting in-depth on 'The Cause of the oppressed People of Sudan'. The SPLM was becoming the flavour of the moment.

Their image outside Africa was rising, and many began to understand the complexities of the underpinning issues regarding the historical discrimination and "double apartheid" of Sudan. Yes, in Garang's words, it was double apartheid! It was racial AND religious discrimination.

Negotiations and jousting with the old boys was a day to day part of my life. I just dealt with it. However, there were also adventures!!

In September 1999, Dr Garang was invited to Norway, Sweden, Denmark, and Finland. It was the highest-level meeting in the history of the SPLM. At the time, I was in the Nuba Mountains doing some research on women's and girls' rights for my book: "Overcoming Gender Conflict and Bias: The Case of New Sudan Women and Girls".

Garang wanted me to accompany him to Scandinavia. He sent a message to the late hero Commander Yusuf Kuwa Mekki (the leader of the Nuba People), requesting that I return back to Nairobi immediately.

However, all Nuba airstrips were effectively closed by Bashir's government. They had placed anti-aircraft units near each to thwart planes landing or taking off. I was stranded.

Dr Garang stated be would wait for my return as long as he possibly could. Commander Kuwa decided we must go by foot. So, we did!

The Nuba Mountains are exactly that...mountains! We had no choice but to climb many of them as the plains were infested with landmines. Being mindful of Khartoum's traps, we managed to creatively pick our way through, avoiding the mines. It took three long weeks of trekking from 3am to till 5pm daily.

Breaks were few. When we could, we rested, ate, and slept.

After running out of drinking water, we relied on rainwater whenever we could find it. Walking through the night was the most difficult part. There were wild animals everywhere. Many a time I found myself stepping into a den of some kind. We were not permitted to use flashlights, lest we attract government soldiers. Being captured and/or killed was not in our plans thank you!

I am ever grateful to the Commander. He was most humble, and one of the kindest leaders I could imagine. He made sure I was safe and accompanied me personally to Panyagor in Upper Nile, Southern Sudan. From there I took a flight bound to Lokichoggio, and then to Nairobi.

I miss you greatly Yusuf Kuwa. I owe you my life and miss your endearing personality. It was too tragic that we lost you after your final battle with cancer.

I arrived in Nairobi and was met by the SPLM Administrator, the late Martin Okerruk. He grabbed my passport and told me he was off to the Swiss Ambassador's home that night. Other ambassadors were gathered there as well. All were anxiously awaiting my arrival, so they could facilitate my Scandinavian visas.

By midnight, Mr Okerruk called me and said I had to be at Jomo Kenyatta International Airport by 6am the following day. Our mission to Scandinavia also included Mama Rebecca Nyandeng de Mabior (Dr Garang's wife), and Deng Alor (the SPLM Foreign Secretary).

Instead of flying directly on KLM from Nairobi to Amsterdam, we travelled via Nigeria to avoid Sudanese airspace. Dr Garang was the most wanted man in the region and a prime target.

In Nigeria, while waiting for our outbound flight to Amsterdam, we met with the then Nigerian President Olusegun Obasanjo. We had a brief, warm discussion. Later, we proceeded to the Netherlands, and then to Oslo, Norway.

Dr Garang was the guest of honour at the Norwegian People's Aid, 60th Anniversary Gala. He was a key speaker! The hall held about 200 global NPA representatives worldwide.

They listened intently and were quite moved while hearing about the suffering of our people. This was their first time facing the facts in a raw, uncensored manner. It triggered an outpouring of emotion.

Mr Halle Jorn, the former NPA Secretary-General could not help shedding tears. As did Ms Hilda Johnson, the ruling Green Party minister for overseas development. Norway affirmed solidarity with the oppressed people of Sudan on that day. It is worth noting, Norwegian humanitarian NGOs such as NPA and Norwegian Christian Aid, NCA had since the 1970s had been assisting South Sudan along humanitarian services. Norway was not a stranger to South Sudan's suffering.

We moved on to Sweden, Denmark, and Finland. The same scenario of shock, disbelief, and yes, guilt. Guilt for standing by all those years without hearing the cries of the oppressed people of Sudan.

I learned a great deal listening to Dr Garang's eloquent, factual and moving narration of our struggle. I became convinced that I made the right decision in joining the movement.

Often, and for reasons best known to him, Dr Garang asked me to add my viewpoint when he was speaking. He did the same when briefing Scandinavian ministers, the media, and others.

While in Europe, the Americans called upon us to visit the USA. This was during President Bill Clinton's administration. We met with his staff in the White House. We never saw the President but met with Dr Susan Rice and other White House administration officials. After a series of questions that we answered forthrightly and honestly, they too were moved.

A couple of months later President Clinton passed an act, The Sudan Peace Act, banning and deregistering any western based oil company that continued operating in Sudan. Anything associated with Bashir was also to be deregistered from the New York Stock Exchange. This was a very powerful course of action. The US is probably the only country in the world with that kind of clout.

A few months later, Dr Rice decided to visit both the south and north of Sudan. In her report to the President, she clearly recommended that the USA urgently involve itself in Sudan's conflict and help to resolve it. She added that the north and the south had virtually become two separate countries given the disparity in development she personally witnessed.

We returned to Africa via Nigeria. By then the late Muammar Gaddafi of Libya had organized an all Africa summit in Sirte, scheduled to begin in September 1999. The Organization of African Unity, the OAU met, and the birth of the African Union, the AU was proclaimed there. Gaddafi also asked Nigerian President Obasanjo to request that Dr Garang visit Libya and meet with him.

Off to Libya we went. Our meeting was a very interesting one. It was in the desert. In a tent. At night. Typical Gaddafi style.

They held their talks in the presence of Eritrea's President Isaias Afwerke. Discussions involved Gaddafi's pledge of full support to the SPLM, and to the people of South Sudan. This was a major shift in policy from his prior position. We were accommodated and generously hosted by the SPLM representative to Libya, commander Edward Lino Abyei.

What a great man he was. Dr Garang did not own a suit and was due to meet Gaddafi. So, Edward lent him his blazer. It was a couple of sizes too small. No matter! He wore it anyway.

We ended our meetings well. Then, Egyptian President Hosni

Mubarak requested that Dr Garang visit him as we "were in the neighbourhood." The meetings with Egyptian leadership, as well as our South Sudanese communities in Egypt, were also constructive.

Egypt also committed to more educational scholarships for South Sudanese students.

We then took the safe route back to Nigeria and returned to Nairobi. A journey of one month became 3 months. A great success!

The SPLM was no longer being regarded as a rebel group. It was now seen as a liberation movement with a genuine cause to free the oppressed. Thusly, we were able to fully expose the regime of President Omar Al Bashir, and its discriminatory policies against the non-Islamic people of Sudan.

The north was now under pressure to negotiate. Several agreements came to pass as a result.

Back at home, there was always more work.

Over and above my unfettered commitment not to back down, I also logged the shortcomings of the old boys' network. I carefully documented their weaknesses and bullying style. This required maneuvering around delicately. I had to avoid butting heads with them. All the while I had to refrain myself from getting to the point of throwing in the towel for good.

As such, I kept totally silent during plenaries but was armed with a notepad and a pen. Laptops were not affordable then. Besides, who am I to show up looking all modern while they could not operate even basic technology. I decided to make life as simple and friction-free as I could. If I had any burning points to push, I would find a way.

This was the time was when we began formulating the political framework for the basis of the peace agreement. The subsequent six protocols we drafted were signed over a period of 3-4 years.

One document was very satisfying to me. Late 2002 saw a protocol signed regarding a cessation of hostilities. This was crucial in order to guarantee safe-haven for civilians who were being targeted by aerial bombardment, helicopter gunship attacks, and frontline fighting. Finally, and at long last, the civilians of South Sudan would be spared.

The old soldiers taught me well regarding the history of our struggle. Of its pain, losses, and sacrifices. Yes, they were extremely gracious in narrating this part, and have my utmost thanks.

As well they were very proficient at ensuring we did not sign an agreement that could have similar pitfalls, as were contained in the Addis Ababa agreement.

They supplied information that was extremely helpful to all of us. I am heavily indebted to them for that. As always, the motto "once beaten, twice shy" resonated throughout.

They fully committed to bringing forth a peace agreement that would be dynamic and relevant in today's world. I tried my best to fit in. However, knowing their egos, I also fully utilized Dr Garang's dynamic brain. I had numerous discussions with him. We conversed about issues in depth, and it helped me prepare at a higher level.

We delved into esoteric items, such as developing a timeline for political frame-works as a guaranteed schedule that must be followed.

To me, that was a commitment. For example, we included the holding of a consensus ahead of the first regional general elections for Southern Sudan. This would provide a framework for the Referendum, so it would be held on schedule.

You see, the whole essence of the agreement for South Sudan was to reach the goal of deciding our fate through a referendum. This desire had been simmering since 1947, at the famous "Juba Conference".

Other issues Dr Garang and I discussed in-depth and agreed upon were: Before holding elections, we would need a multi-party democracy system in place. The SPLM should not be the only party.

Freedom of the media and unrestricted movement of the people must be guaranteed. We envisioned a vibrant empowered civil society. One that, together with the would-be Government of Southern Sudan and international organizations, could join hands and ensure maximum civic education.

With an illiteracy rate of over 90% in an entity that never had held elections before, we had an uphill task. We absolutely needed to ensure our people understood the requirement for a census and general elections.

With these sorts of open practical discussions, Dr Garang and I were able to team up on the issues. This ensured that the old guard would accept such dynamic change.

As well, we managed to discuss in depth the need for good governance in the interim period by a provisional SPLM-led government. Required also was the inclusion of civil society experts in the drafting process of the Interim Constitution.

Built into the Comprehensive Peace Agreement (CPA) being worked on we had a 6-month pre-interim period, whereby we could draft an Interim Constitution and process it for review.

In a sense, Dr Garang was my ace in the hole. I also had another one up my sleeve. I never stopped working with the NESI Network, and other civil society activists. We continued to perform lobby and advocacy work for peace and human rights, as well as empowering local communities.

Regarding a working peace agreement, our aim was to get very close to the media. This would ensure our 'agenda' was also reckoned with. We would write demands and petitions regarding inclusions that we wanted to see in any peace agreement.

Our prime media focus was on television. I would usually wear my negotiator hat. On camera, I would hand over documents to key figures such as Kenyan Chief Mediator General Lazarus Sumbiywu, SPLM chief negotiator Nhial Deng Nhial, and the Sudan Government chief negotiators (their names varied over time from Nafie Ali Nafie, to Mutrif, and others).

Our visual media assault "embarrassed" the opposing parties negotiators. A beneficial side-effect of our approach was that we attracted the attention of the International Partners Forum (USA, UK, Norway, Netherlands, Italy and Canada).

That's how I delicately worked alongside the old boys. I gave them my utmost respect and listened to them endlessly. I made sure they were aware that I wrote down their historical narration of the Struggle. Every time I felt isolated or shunned by them, I saluted them for their selfless sacrifices and told them how enriching it was for me to learn from them.

Gradually, some of them began appreciating my patience and level of endurance. I also noted some interesting practices regarding guerrilla/liberation movements. They would be quite harsh and almost rude to newcomers, especially women.

They deliberately try to test you to see if you were tough, or would just quit. An observation I took note of very keenly was that every time I did something well, they would go silent and seem almost appreciative. But they never said it out loud. Then when they wanted to test my resilience, they talked to me harshly and dismissed my ideas.

My prime focus was ensuring that human rights and democratic principles were enshrined in the agreement. I had to persevere and had to utilize creative channels to back me up.

The most important thing I learned is to NEVER give up when facing such rigidity. Find ways to work with the like-minded to help you to form alliances and back you up. As well, if the leader is visionary and dynamic, ensure he or she hears you directly. Your agenda must be clear, consistent and viable! A young woman with the right vision, agenda and strategies 'can' work alongside older, rigid-minded individuals. This helps not only ensure goal achievement but also helps to transform mindsets.

In the end, it all helped forge the agreement.

After the signing, Dr Garang appointed 5 Interim Constitution drafting commissioners. I was the only female and youngest member. The committee had multiple assignments and a deadline.

As commissioners, we undertook our work as per our appointment. We handed Dr Garang the Constitution in May 2005, at Rumbek, Southern Sudan. He was very grateful. The document was crucial, so he could set up his semi-autonomous Southern Sudan Government, as per the terms of the peace agreement, by July 2005.

However, first, he had to be sworn in as Sudan's First Vice President in Khartoum by his then President Omar Al Bashir, also per the agreement.

On Tuesday, July 14, 2005, I had my very last one-on-one meeting with Dr John Garang. He had offered me a ministerial post (he also gave me the choice in which ministry I thought I would serve best). As well, he gave me the option of either working in his soon-to-be Juba or Khartoum-based governments per the CPA. The choice rested on me, he said. I took a deep breath, and we discussed it all at length.

I told him we both knew that the Bashir's government did not sign in good faith. The roadway of the 6-year interim period would be filled with superficial thorns and obstacles. It was best I remained outside government, and focus on NESI/ civil society matters to counter any violations from an independent standpoint.

Besides that, I also had my 4-year-old son to think about. I had shared with him my single motherhood frustrations during the entire period of the IGAD-facilitated Sudan peace process. Now I needed time to be away from mainstream politics.

I simply needed to dedicate time to my son, Dritayi. Dr Garang placed my son on his lap and looked deep into my eyes. He said, "Suzanne, I totally understand." It was a two-and-a-half-hour meeting. Little did I know it would be my last time to see him alive.

On Friday, July 15, 2005, Dr Garang left Nairobi on a flight bound to Khartoum. He was to be sworn in the following day. Hundreds of thousands, including South Sudanese, Nuba, Funj, and even Arab Sudanese, showed up at the airport to meet a hero. Khartoum's streets were filled. There was no space for even bicycles to pass.

On Saturday the swearing-in ceremony attracted even larger crowds. It was like the whole of Sudan converged on Khartoum to meet their saviour. Every oppressed person could relate to him. He was the man to lead them to justice, equality, and liberty. Dr

John Garang was duly sworn in as the First Vice President of Sudan under President Omar Al Bashir. It also essentially made him the President of South Sudan.

By Sunday, July 17th, 2005 he had returned to Nairobi and began preparations to go to Juba. He was a very busy man at that point. World leaders were calling him. There were interviews for the media. As well communicated with his colleagues, family, and friends.

He was invited by Ugandan President Yoweri Museveni to visit him in Mbarara (Museveni's hometown) to discuss mutual issues. The two leaders were great friends.

The meeting ended well, and Dr Garang flew out in Museveni's own helicopter. The flight was bound for New Site, a border town between South Sudan and Kenya.

However, according to various unconfirmed reports, the aircraft was mysteriously diverted to Entebbe, then New Site. Daylight was running out, and the destination airstrip was only makeshift, without lights or a tower.

His wife was waiting for him there.

At last, around 7pm, the sound of an aircraft was heard over the skies of New Site. Everyone rushed to the airstrip to receive their leader. But the craft did not land. Instead, it flew on. Minutes passed. Suddenly, the people on the ground heard a loud bang. Then complete silence.

It was Saturday evening of July 30th, 2005.

The residents of New Site went to see what was wrong. At about 5am they finally located the crushed remains that carried Dr John Garang. All on board were dead. It was early morning of Sunday, July 31, 2005. He was no more! The World woke up to the shocking news. It was a far cry from the happiness of 9th

January, when the peace agreement was signed. That day, the 30th of July 2005 remains a most tragic and painful day in the history of South Sudan. The day we lost Dr John Garang.

Former UN Secretary-General, Mr Kofi Anan appeared on CNN, with tears in his eyes saying, "Dr Garang was larger than life." The BBC, CNN, AP, Radio France, plus many more African, and world news media outlets, had dreams of condolences. It was all mixed with the creeping fear that Southern Sudan had not only lost Garang, but possibly any political gains made to date. Most felt the likely outcome would be a reversion to war until further notice.

The fear was real, and the shock was overwhelming. The pain of his loss was too much for many to comprehend. A candle was put out. A rose died, as did our dreams and aspirations. It felt totally hopeless.

To this date, we do not know whether it was an assassination or an accident. We all mourned and were crushed. The fear of losing his vision and the gains toward peace became a grim reality. We panicked!

However, by necessity, our determination was revitalized within days. This was ably led by his widow Mama Rebecca Nyandeng de Mabior. She told us that her husband's vision lived in each and every one of us. We MUST not give up. That truly saved the day. Her iron-willed message echoed in all corners of the land.

Within a short period of time, we wiped our tears and carried on.

I mourned for months. I mourn to this day. He was a father figure to me. A mentor, a coach, and the one who shoved me into politics. His memory shall forever live on. I will always be grateful for the opportunity of having worked very closely with him. We spent seven intensive years on extremely important issues. Rest in peace my comrade, mentor, and friend.

Return to Khartoum

Do I miss Khartoum? This question was put to a test in July 2005. In order to sign the Comprehensive Peace Agreement, Dr Garang was expected to travel to Khartoum as previously mentioned for the signing ceremony. This after more than 22 years of fighting the regime of President Bashir. Dr Garang was still the most wanted man in Sudan for being the leader of the rebellion movement. As part of the team, I was also expected to accompany him.

I was TERRIFIED!

Obviously, I was considered a rebel having been a part of SPLM/A since 1998. I was also a wanted person.

Did I believe the regime to be genuine about peace and about treating us as equals? NO!

Were my childhood promises to never return to Khartoum in my mind? YES!! Many emotions raged inside me.

However, even after the death of Dr Garang, Khartoum wasn't done with me yet. In July 2008, I received an email from the SPLM, requesting that I return to Juba to meet with its Chairman, President Salva Kiir. I was asked to accept the SPLM foreign secretary post to pave the way for building foreign relations. We were nearing the end of the CPA period, and the completion of our Referendum for our destiny as free people.

I agreed and went to Juba and began my duties. Being a national secretary, I was required to be based in Khartoum as well as Juba.

I dreaded that with every fibre of my being!

My first decision was to commute to Khartoum when I was needed, instead of being based there.

I would only travel for meetings with foreign ambassadors etc. that were stationed in the north.

It frightened me to go.

In fact, I vividly remember the very first time I boarded a flight to Khartoum, in February 2009. It was only a few months after taking the oath of office. I dreaded each passing second. I simply did not want to go to that awful place!

Then the realization dawned on me that I was completely traumatized by my childhood memories. I never could feel welcomed in Khartoum again. At the first hotel I stayed in, it seemed all eyes were upon me. I felt scrutinized in every movement I made. Thereafter, I utilized extra security measures. I would check into any hotel in Khartoum, but would secretly stay with family members still living there.

I would always travel in different cars and had a separate laptop from the one I would use in Juba. My "Khartoum laptop" had nothing in it. I never carried any separate storage disk drives or anything that could have any value or vital information.

I SIMPLY DID NOT TRUST ANYONE IN KHARTOUM.

Sadly, I did not have any urge to visit any of our old Moslem neighbourhood friends. I feared being followed. That might subject them to scrutiny by Bashir's government agents.

That is when I truly realized South Sudan would separate. If I, who grew up in Khartoum could feel this disconnected and unwelcome, what about the millions of South Sudanese who never lived there? Not to mention those who fled fearing for their lives!

All so sad really. An invisible painful chapter in my childhood that was stolen from me by misguided imposition and assimilation attempts. Not just by the government but increasingly by the ordinary Moslems of Khartoum.

We cannot yet heal together as people who once lived side and be good peaceful neighbours. We carry a lot of silent hurt and bitterness that is yet to be discussed openly. I hope to live long enough to see that day.

Fulfilling my role properly meant ensuring to meet with all heads of foreign missions in both Juba and Khartoum, briefing them. As well, I listened to and took their advice and criticism regarding the SPLM.

Many a time, I travelled to Khartoum with my son, Dritayi. The foreign ambassadors were great. From green tea served by the Chinese ambassador, to colouring pens and paper by the French ambassador, to sweets by the USA charge d'affairs, to kids jokes told by the EU representative (who also doubled up as the Dutch Ambassador), to good old Kenyan chai (tea) offered to my son by their Ambassador.

I simply had to explain that being away from my son for more than a day or two was just too unbearable for both the little boy and myself as a single parent. They fully understood and sympathized with us. My boy was wonderful. He quietly sat in a corner trying to follow some of the discussions and fell asleep during longer meetings. It was all very sweet and fulfilling to a loving mother who is also committed to serving her country. I could not have asked for more!

These personal meetings with the ambassadors contributed significantly toward trust-building and restoration of hope for the SPLM. I was patient when it was severely criticized. I never disputed their claims or argued. I knew the ambassadors spoke the painful truth. So, when I began developing the first SPLM foreign policy guidelines, these ambassadors became my 'indirect consultants'. I used their vast expertise and hands-on knowledge to help me draft and develop policy. I listened to their expectations regarding South Sudan once it became an independent country, and how they envisaged to develop diplomatic relations with this soon to be nation.

I also engaged with the SPLM and ordinary South Sudanese regarding their expectations, aspirations, and desires. In the end, I managed to function in a city that had caused me such pain. Facing my fears made me stronger.

The Salva Kiir Years

The first time I met Mr Kiir was in August 1999, at New Kush, Southern Sudan during the first SPLM Women's Conference.

It was a most historical event, with about 700 delegates from all over Southern Sudan, the Nuba Mountains, and the Southern Blue Nile region (the Funj people). By 1998 the movement had been in existence for about 15 years. During this time, it was able to liberate extensive areas of Sudan.

Since 1994, the SPLM held a series of conventional administrative workshops that were different from most other liberation movements. During that year it held its first Civil Authority of New Sudan (CANS) convention. A declaration was made that it was time to return all liberated areas from military to civilian rule.

By proclaiming the area controlled by the SPLM as "New Sudan", it was underpinning the ideology of a new political dispensation. This was a viewpoint diametrically opposed to the "old" Sudan, which was marred by slavery, discrimination, and oppression.

THE SALVA KIIR YEARS

In 1996, the SPLM held its first civil society conference, calling upon all civilians to form such groups. This was viewed from outside as the SPLM trying to reform itself as an organization. It was also seen as introducing "new" concepts to the extremely isolated, forgotten, and little-known region.

By 1997, the movement which began as a socialist-communist organisation acknowledged that the people of Southern Sudan and other marginalized areas have different beliefs and faiths. That the SPLM must respect those differences.

At this point, they called for an All Faiths conference. Two new 'faith-based' institutions were established. The New Sudan Council of Churches (NSCC), and the New Sudan Islamic Council. This made the SPLM even more popular among the people. By August 1998 the SPLM, under the visionary leadership of Dr John Garang, decided that the women needed to be heard. Their voices were to be formulated into policy.

He assigned me to help organize a women's conference. The overwhelming demand to attend was amazing. You could feel and see it in almost every woman's face. Young and old alike! This was their day!

Traditional leaders, elders and community groups were also invited to provide their valuable input.

Mr Salva Kiir was present during the event. I took note that he listened attentively but never uttered a word during the entire seven days. We concluded the conference with unanimous agreement on women's demands for justice, human rights, and equality.

I was mandated to draft a policy for it. The delegates returned to their respective destinations. I went back to Nairobi and immediately fired up my laptop to start extrapolating conference resolutions into policy. Within four days the draft was ready.

Together with the Mama Keziah Lainywa, the former SPLM Gender and Child Welfare Secretary, we arranged to meet Mr Kiir in the Nairobi SPLM office.

Once there, we would hand over both the Resolutions and the Policy.

The soft-spoken Mr Kiir warmly welcomed us into his office. He had a small notepad and a pen. I noticed that he kept writing down anything either Mama Keziah or myself said. We handed him both documents, exchanged pleasantries and left.

With the series of SPLM organizational reforms and societal restructuring (governance) taking shape between 19941998, life began to have some semblance of normalcy. Almost!

Years passed, and I never heard from or saw Mr Kiir until July 2002. It was in Machakos, Kenya.

He was assigned by Dr Garang to sign the Political Framework, known as the Machakos Protocol. It was part of a series to be signed before the final peace agreement.

Once more, years passed before I saw him. Between 2002-2005, I continued my work participating in peace talks and fulfilling my NESI Network duties.

The Comprehensive Peace Agreement was signed in January 2005 in Nairobi.

As covered in other chapters, on July 16, 2005, Dr Garang was sworn in as the first Vice President of the Republic of Sudan. By the 30th of that same month, he was dead. He never lived to form his government.

It was important not to have a leadership vacuum given such a volatile situation. The SPLM leadership met within four days

THE SALVA KIIR YEARS

of the tragic event. They decided that Mr Salva Kiir Mayardiit would take over the leadership. He would fill in the gap as he was Dr Garang's deputy.

On Wednesday, August 3, 2005, Mr Kiir was sworn in as the President of the semi-autonomous government of Southern Sudan. Life went on, though we all mourned for a long time.

President Kiir formed his government in November of that same year. Life seemed to be headed in a good way. I carried on working with the NESI Network empowering communities through civic education, basic social services and capacity building. We always remained vigilant to any violations of the peace agreement. Often, we compiled reports on the CPA's progress, presenting discussions, and organizing orientation meetings.

Basically, NESI tried its best to keep the world informed that the CPA was not the end result. Rather, it was a 6-year interim period journey whereby certain provisions were to be carried out. Items such as the first general elections, various referendums. and other major political activities were on the agenda. The SPLM, by virtue of signing the CPA, became the liberating and ruling party of the semi-autonomous regional Southern Sudan government (GOSS) from 2005-2011. As I wrote in "The Garang Years" chapter, he wanted to nominate me to be a minister either in Juba or Khartoum. Dr Garang was like a father and a mentor to me. He helped build me up politically.

However, prior to his death, I told him I wanted out of government.

It was time to be on the 'outside' for a while.

More importantly, I needed to dedicate time to my 4-year-old son. I hardly had any time for him, as I was overly engaged in public work leading up to the signing. So, I took a break from active politics.

The CPA had been signed, and I could now focus on both my son and the NESI Network. I would monitor the peace agreement implementation, as well as to continue to empower our local communities. I kept away from politics 2005-2008. It was GREAT being with my son, and with like-minded civil society community activists.

By mid-2008, the SPLM started organizing and preparing itself. After all, they had been administering the liberated areas of Southern Sudan for more than 20 years. Everyone knew and believed in them.

It was and still is, a tough time for the other political parties to survive. It doesn't matter how noble the vision, or beneficial the programmes these political parties may have. The SPLM is the one and only group the people locally and internationally recognised.

The SPLM held its convention in May 2008, per its constitution. It required mandates on various political issues. These included the upcoming elections and the referendum.

During this Convention, they decided to create a foreign relations secretariat and to nominate a competent secretary to establish and manage it. In the past, the SPLM only had an ad-hoc foreign relations secretary with no constitutional job description.

They decided that even though Sudan remained one country, there was a regional government of Southern Sudan, and it must have governmental functionality.

Foreign policy and relations were all conducted by and reflected the outlook of Khartoum's Arab/Islamic base.

Furthermore, the CPA's 6-year interim period provided for two options:

North and South Sudan would remain united, or Southern Sudan through a referendum may opt for total independence from North Sudan.

Most Southern Sudanese yearned for their independence. The SPLM knew this. But the two entities were still one. Hence, they could not have parallel foreign affairs ministries and embassies. The only option would be to establish a foreign relations docket through the SPLM. Its political bureau board of directors met in July 2008 and deliberated upon the earlier Convention resolutions. Three names were floated to establish the proposed SPLM foreign relations secretariat. My name was one of them and garnered the most votes. Mr Kiir, the chairperson, requested that the SPLM Secretary General Mr Pagan Amoum inform me of this decision.

Around this time, both my son and I were on a family leave. My older sister, Mary had tragically died in a car crash in Canada in November 2007. She left behind her two-year-old daughter Velisha, and her husband. I was only able to attend the burial in 2007. Then I had to rush back to Africa to be with my young son who was left alone with the nanny.

Dritayi and I wanted to spend a month with my orphaned niece, Velisha in Calgary, Canada. I also wanted to spend some time with our Mother in Atlanta, Georgia (USA). Family time. Something we all badly needed.

This is one of the most painful aspects of war. It scatters families around the globe. Many a time we are never able to attend burials or be around our sick loved ones. Birthdays and special moments are lost. Separations decades in length is the norm for many thousands of South Sudanese and other war scattered peoples. Such is the painful life of a refugee. Let me add that this includes refugees from famine, floods and the multitude of other natural disasters that strike the planet.

Like most of the modern world, and although on a family holiday, I always kept tabs on my emails. I received one Mr Amoum's email regarding the appointment.

He asked if I could make my way to Juba as soon as possible to meet with the SPLM leadership to discuss the details.

I replied I was on family leave and the earliest I could return to Africa was the end of August. I also had a prior engagement discussing a paper on Transitional Justice in Cape Town, South Africa in early September.

Once we got back to Kenya, and after reflection and consultation with my younger brother Jambo Jr., I decided to take the role. However, there would be some conditions attached.

On October 11, 2008, I travelled to Juba and met with President Kiir. We spoke for over three hours.

I laid out my conditions.

These included: acceptance that my son is my priority, always; my independence regarding speaking my opinion; and my commitment to the work of civil society and human rights.

Mr Kiir accepted.

Then, he shared some alarming insights. Mr Kiir said (and I already knew this) that the SPLM reputation was on the line. It was extremely corrupt, and as a result, this may affect the completion of the general elections, as well as the referendum as laid out in the CPA.

He further stated that the national agenda was almost forgotten, and personal interests were everything. He cautioned me to be very careful, and that my work was critical if we were to improve the badly tarnished image of the SPLM nationally, regionally, and internationally.

He added that he was fully aware of some elements in SPLM hierarchy who turned their "liberation" values into business ventures. Ones driven by selfish interests at the expense of the people of Southern Sudan.

I was stunned. The SPLM is now known as the party of corruption?

He warned me that I would be faced with challenges and obstacles in carrying out my work, by these elements. This part shocked me, and I found myself torn between accepting the role or backing off. However, Mr Kiir was quick to notice this and emphasized that if I did not take on this task, most likely the South would fail in its foreign relations. Then, far more negative implications, including our failure to conduct the referendum timely may arise. The goal was to rebuild the broken trust between the SPLM and the world community, Mr Kiir said. He guilt-tripped me like a pro. National duty called! I decided there and then that I would take up the challenge and give it my best shot.

The president assured me of his assistance and offered free access to him whenever I needed moral support or advice.

His number one message was that he wished South Sudan could export peace to the world. He said that since we were so familiar with war and its consequences, we were well suited to counsel others on the benefits of peace.

Now that I had accepted the role, it was critical that a plan was formulated. I researched online regarding other countries' foreign policies. I was rather shocked to find out there were several African countries with no written foreign policy at all. Some had been independent for decades!

My laptop was my indispensable friend in the office, in meetings, conferences, my bedroom, airport lounges, and on planes. I carried on tapping away no matter where I was. I did not want to miss out on any ideas. Not even one! Ours was soon to be the world's newest nation!

Our people had endured selfless sacrifices and painful tragedies of all types, including deprivation of such basic freedoms as the right to exist as human beings. I dreamt of a "state of the art" nation, and a country that would be most grateful to its friends in the world.

I imagined there would be potential new partnerships to start the foreign relations ball rolling, with a vision to develop South Sudan equally and equitably.

No more yearnings and sufferings for South Sudanese when it came to education, acquiring skills, technology, infrastructure etc. A wise, transparent, environmentally friendly, and pro-future generations foreign policy. That was my dream and it was based on listening to everyone I could.

On October 13, 2008, I was sworn in as the SPLM national external relations secretary. It was an organization in shambles. Even their office space was a joke. I was given a small cubicle. No computer. No laptop. But I did have a huge Toyota Land Cruiser V8 at my disposal. This SHOCKED me! How as part of a liberation movement in a post-conflict Southern Sudan, where there are no roads or infrastructure, and abject poverty all over, can the SPLM afford this exorbitant mindless expense? This huge monstrosity of a vehicle! I stormed into the office of my immediate boss, the Mr Amoum. I was furious and shaking with rage.

He calmed me down, asked me to sit, and tried lamely to explain that since I was the national foreign secretary (equivalent to a government minister) I was entitled to such a vehicle. I found myself loudly complaining that we were liberators, not royalty!

Luxurious, extremely expensive cars are not for liberators. There is no way I would attend a public rally arriving in such a car. After all, there was no public transport, and most likely our constituents would arrive on foot. How disgusting would it be that the so-called "liberators" like myself would step out of such an expensive vehicle? It would be completely against the principle of equality.

He went quiet, and I took his shrug to mean 'take it or leave it'. I walked out of his office wondering what I had gotten myself into. So, over the next several years I found myself acting like those the I protested against! Should I have refused? Possibly. Maybe. Probably. I consoled myself by reasoning that I would make this vehicle work extremely hard, and I would do my best to serve my country, and my people. However, the whole episode saddened me.

One can only conclude that this type of dysfunction added to the failures of the SPLM as a governing body. In turn, it fractured the management of the country, thusly bringing it to its knees today.

Almost the entire so-called SPLM senior cadres were clueless and refused to learn. They had no desire to implement the principles of justice, equality, and liberty.

I came to the swift realization that the administration department had no idea whatsoever regarding organization. The political affairs department had no political work! There were no political engagements with SPLM's vast membership.

Nothing to exchange, inform, or update the constituencies. Nothing in place as a feedback mechanism to hear from them of what they, as members, thought of the SPLM.

Somehow that was supposed to be balanced by the ready availability of lots of cups of tea and friendly visitors. We would sit from 9am to 5pm sitting,

chatting and doing nothing. One week of that was enough to last a lifetime! Not my style! I searched for a pc, a laptop, office supplies, and flash drives using my own resources. I get a monster vehicle, but nothing for the office! No internet!

What a joke. The SPLM was out of its depth regarding administrative issues. No thought was given to a website and decent publications to inform the public or the world. No way to connect at all! I could not believe my eyes!

So, I used my private email address and began building a database of contacts nationally, regionally, and worldwide. To make matters worse, as foreign secretary I did not have any budget whatsoever to travel and connect with anyone.

Next, I embarked on developing my work plan. I began by fermenting annual action plans encompassing activities on how to engage with political parties inside and outside Sudan. This included engaging with the SPLM South Sudanese, the almost two million Diaspora, and to revitalize the movement's foreign relations by engaging on daily basis with the few consulates located in Juba.

Also, whenever possible, I travelled to Khartoum to meet with Northern political parties and foreign embassies. But I could not do the work alone. Neither could the work be done without a constitutionally-mandated work plan.

I began creating posts and job descriptions accordingly.

This role would normally be facilitated by a human resources department. However, I assumed the job myself. No time to waste!

I was able to create three deputy posts. They were to be responsible for foreign relations, political parties, and the Diaspora. This was enacted under my constitutional job description as the external secretary. Thereupon, I created directorates along the same three thematic areas.

Next, I began working on policies to operationalize the constitutional mandate.

I worked from the bottom up. Through a series of meetings and emails, with pre-developed questionnaires, I was able to formulate an actual agenda regarding foreign policy and diaspora guidelines. Yes, it was the first in the history of the SPLM!

I was able to do all this without external support from professionals. Obviously, I did not work alone. I also had no approved budget, to help facilitate to develop these policies. This is despite my numerous written proposals.

The way the SPLM was managed was beyond comedic. Buying luxury vehicles was a priority. Facilitating funding for policy, program development, and actual work was given no consideration at all.

You had to fend for yourself if you needed anything done! I earned a salary and had an expensive vehicle (fuelled weekly) and that was it!

I shall always be grateful to my former national external secretariat team: the late Alesio Clement on Diaspora issues, Mr Mohamed on political issues, and to Dr Peter Lam, Luc Kang, Helen Denya, Tariq Aziz, Tongun Farajalla and Ms Aziza Mohamed and the rest. I thank them all for their dedication and genuine willingness to learn, adapt, and work professionally. I was always travelling from one country to another for meetings and conferences while they ran the show on the ground in both Juba and Khartoum.

I fell back on my civil society network and I doubled up working both as foreign secretary and with NESI. That's how I could travel to over twenty countries worldwide.

I used personal connections to meet with regional and international foreign officials to promote the work of the SPLM for a country yet to be born. I had to use charm and keep them interested in South Sudan.

I chose an honest and frank approach. Whenever foreign government officials accused the SPLM of corruption and produced facts and names, I never denied any of it. However, I asked them to help us make right what is wrong. Then, they began to warm up to me. After all, I was always accessible. Whatever information they needed, even if it was not within my docket, I made sure to help and connect them to the right channel. I found myself becoming the "focal" point of Southern Sudan.

Most government and SPLM officials in Juba hardly used the internet, if at all. Often, they never answered their phones. I worked around the clock to regain lost trust. My greatest fear was of our people being thrust yet again into war. The rest of the world MUST endorse our 2011 referendum outcome.

I worked with President Kiir very closely. He was always a mystery. You either liked him for his humble demeanour or hated him for never talking. "What is going on in his mind?" was always the overriding question of anyone after meeting him. I often thought I knew him well, but equally doubted whether I really knew him at all!

For over 8 years I met with him virtually on a weekly basis, and usually for no less than one hour. I appointed myself to be on the lookout for anything shifty going on. I genuinely, and very honestly (perhaps somewhat naively) checked, and counter-checked, most external and internal political developments. Then, I advised him on what I felt was the best course of action.

The amount looted by the SPLM between 2006-2009 is claimed to have been about four billion US dollars. There was no accountability whatsoever. Not even receipts or vouchers. The money was simply drawn out and used by various senior SPLM luminaries and ministers. None of this worked its way down to the people. It seems they were simply born to suffer.

I knew of all this. But who am I to do anything?

Any attempt to persecute or take anyone to court would be inviting certain death.

Which courts or judges would dare to stand against the face of these dangerous ex-guerrilla fighters, now fully entrenched in powerful positions in both the SPLM and the Government.

I reached out to President Kiir. After all, he assured me of his support whenever I was stuck. I shared all my concerns with him.

How could I improve the image of SPLM internationally when the SPLM leaders are such major thieves? He looked at me, went quiet for a moment, and told me he knew of the theft taking place in his government, and within the SPLM.

I was extremely angry hearing that, and asked him: "Why didn't you act?"

He calmly answered that if he did that prior to our 2011 referendum, the peace agreement would be shattered, and we would lose our hard-won gains. He convinced me that our priority was to hang on as best we could. Accountability for the public fund's theft would be the first priority once we gained our independence. This actually made some sense, and I agreed to continue.

In late 2008, I decided that to win the world's trust, the SPLM needed to hold an All Sudan Political Parties Conference. We would bring together the northern and southern parties to chart the way forward as a political front. I developed the concept and met with Mr Amoum. He seemed to have liked the idea, and I presented him with both the written proposal and a very humble budget. I told him that I already secured the funding for it by the world community because they were eager for such a political awakening in Sudan.

He promised to study the proposal, and give an answer promptly. Months went by.

I tailed him everywhere to remind him. I met with him in Juba several times over it.

I travelled to both Khartoum and Cairo, following him so he could green-light the project. Time was of the essence.

I gave up the chase after four months and decided to bypass him. I met with President Kiir in February 2009.

I explained to President Kiir that the other parties had always claimed that the CPA was only a bilateral agreement between the SPLM and Bashir's National Congress Party, the NCP.

I told him that all northern traditional, sectarian, historical, and household political parties, such as the UMMA of Sadiq al Mahadi, The Democratic Unionist Party, DUP of Al Merghani, the Communist Party under Ustaz Nugud and other prominent political parties, may feel enabled to disown the Referendum outcome as they never recognized the CPA.

A fix was badly needed. The SPLM was considered a bully in the South! I visited some of the southern Sudanese political leaders in their homes to convince them we needed to open new channels of dialogue. Not an easy task.

Their overwhelming negativity regarding the SPLM powerbase would cause the average person to flee. I could not do that. Instead, I chose to listen and empathize with them. For I knew they spoke honestly about the painful truth and reality of the situation.

On the other hand, we needed the Northern Sudanese political parties on board, and we could dialogue with these formidable parties in a "win-win" arena. Their demands were freedom of expression, economic reforms, and multiparty recognition.

Our agenda was simply to agree to all that while they approved the peace agreement.

President Kiir loved the idea, and as the Chairperson, he immediately ordered the SPLM political bureau hierarchy to pledge its full support for this historic conference.

I named the conference "Toward the Full Implementation of the Comprehensive Peace Agreement".

Miraculously, no one "noticed" or made an objection to the conference theme. All politicians focused on the topics to be discussed, and I accepted 'everything' they recommended while praying silently that they would never notice the meaning behind the name; the fulfilment of the CPA.

IT WORKED! The various political groups within Sudan endorsed it as well.

I began shuttling back and forth between Juba and Khartoum and had meetings with several foreign ambassadors there. Amongst others, they were from the USA, UK, Uganda, Kenya, South Africa, China, Norway, the Netherlands, and other EU countries. They were elated that the SPLM had "woken" up and would begin to work with political parties on issues such as freedom of the press, peace, human rights etc. They offered to assist with transporting and accommodating the politicians from Northern Sudan to Juba.

I then travelled to Norway, met with foreign affairs officials and they gave us full support.

The Conference was a great success! Mr Sadiq Al Mahadi, the first elected prime minister of the Sudan and leader of the traditional UMMA party arrived in Juba for the very first time. So did the late Dr Hassan Turabi, the man believed to have influenced former President Jaafar Numeiri to introduce Islamic Sharia Laws into Sudan in 1983. It was historical!

We also had all the Southern Sudanese parties present. The Juba Declaration fully endorsing the CPA was achieved. We gained the nation's trust. All of it was accomplished very peacefully! Bashir could not oppose the referendum, and the world community began re-gaining its trust in the SPLM.

Needless to add, I believe to this day my former boss and others most likely do not know how I managed to put this conference together. Neither do they know how I was able to achieve the real hidden agenda.

My fear was based on a previous painful experience committed against the Southern Sudanese in 1983 when Numeiri abrogated the 1972 Addis Ababa Peace Agreement, calling it "Neither a Quran or Bible", meaning it can be broken!

Myself, like many millions of other South Sudanese, feared the same could have happened with the new peace agreement. That is why I was so driven to get the utmost commitment of all Sudanese political parties to the CPA.

The conference ended, and the CPA 6-year interim period was also nearing its end. So little time, so much to do.

During our long struggle for freedom, and especially

during the SPLM era, many African countries, international organizations, and individuals stood by us. However, once we signed the CPA, Southern Sudan isolated itself from the world.

SPLM luminaries spent their time looting public funds. Such criminal behaviour disappointed millions of Southern Sudanese and the outside world. That was beyond shameful.

I had to think very hard. How can the SPLM regain the trust of all? That was vital. I began reviewing old contacts. Sadly, some had died, but many were still alive. I approached them. I used humility and honesty in order to gain a hearing. They were far too bitter and angry to listen. Understandably and rightfully so!

One at a time, these friends, countries and organizations began hearing me out. I apologized on SPLM's behalf and reminded them that what mattered most was the innocent people of Southern Sudan. Tempers cooled down.

By end October 2009, I approached President Kiir and advised him that it was crucial that he travel and reconnect with them.

He needed to thank them for their solidarity during our years of struggle and to introduce himself to their leaders.

Critically as well, it would ensure their understanding of his vision for South Sudan.

This was key. Once the Referendum was conducted in 2011, the world community would have already gained some relative confidence in his leadership. The tarnished image of the SPLM would be made slightly more bearable for them.

He hesitated, saying that it was already wintertime in Europe, and he did not trust the weather for flying. However, I managed to convince him. He visited Norway, the Netherlands, the UK, Italy, and France.

This brief diplomatic effort worked, and the 'little known' President Kiir, became a bit more known. He was well received and made a good impression as a humble leader. Gradually, the trust between Southern Sudan and the Western world was coming back.

Upon his return from Europe, there were a lot of issues taking place in Khartoum. Bashir was facing riots all over the north. Panicking, he called President Kiir and asked for his intervention. Apparently, after the Juba All Sudanese Political Parties October 2009 Conference, Northern Sudanese political parties were revived, refreshed, and determined to restore democracy. He asked President Kiir to intervene and calm them down.

Kiir agreed on two conditions:

One would be for President Bashir to provide basic freedoms for all political parties in Sudan.

Secondly, Bashir was to approve the Referendum Act. An act that had been awaiting ratification since 2008.

Fearing an uprising against him, he readily agreed. A win for all. The very best kind of agreement!

Next, I proposed that President Kiir visit South Africa and brief them on the peace process. I accompanied him there with a delegation.

We also journeyed to Botswana, Angola, and Mozambique. He was thus able to thank these countries for their solidarity and support during our years of struggle.

This also guaranteed the "blessing" of these countries, as part of the African Union, to endorse the Referendum outcome forthcoming in 2011. They were extremely grateful for this visit and registered their appreciation. By early December 2009, we returned to Juba and went back to preparation work for the general elections to be held early in 2010.

THE SALVA KIIR YEARS

President Kiir often travelled to Ethiopia, Kenya, and Uganda so there was no urgent need to include these countries. It was an excellent trust building year for the SPLM and Southern Africa region!

Around that time, December 2009, I had to return to South Africa on another mission. The South African-based Institute for Strategic Studies, in conjunction with other think-tank groups in South Africa, worked on other possible outcomes that may occur in South Sudan if things went badly.

Africa's longest civil war was not one to be lightly taken. Nor was fully banking on the CPA, or goodwill by all. We decided to work on all possible scenarios. This needed to be done with the input of the signatories. The SPLM and the NCP of Bashir. December was a tough time, as most wanted to have their year-end break. Both myself and Ms Paula Rouque, the coordinator for the institute at the time, used highly persuasive methods to ensure both parties were in South Africa.

Scenarios were laid out in different forms, including what could happen if the referendum failed, and war broke out again. This was a very useful exercise, and we were able to broaden our thinking regarding possible solutions for any foreseeable scenario. This was equally useful to the African and world communities, as they would need to be alerted in case there was need of intervention on their part.

2010 was a very tightly scheduled year. The general election, and of course immediately thereafter the long-awaited referendum was looming.

As such, Southern Sudan was a beehive of election activities. With no infrastructure, roads, or other means to reach the remote areas, the people were determined nevertheless, to do their duty.

The government directed the South Sudan Census Commission to begin its work. They virtually walked door to door, village to village, conducting the census. It was a binding prerequisite to the March 2010 General elections. Miraculously, they were able to conclude it, and our population estimate was about 12 million South Sudanese. Added to that total were those located in North Sudan and the Diaspora outside the country.

The SPLM and other political parties were focused on identifying their candidates, political programmes, and respective campaign strategies. In just two months the voters would be in the polling stations!

Interestingly, by late February the SPLM political affairs docket had not prepared any campaign programme for its flag bearer and presidential aspirant, the incumbent President Kiir. I was totally confused by that, and so were many other SPLM members. The Party prepared work for all its other candidates including the vice chairperson, governors, and members of parliament in all the ten states of Southern Sudan. All, EXCEPT for its chairperson. INTERESTING!

This became the talk of Juba in political circles. "How divided is the SPLM?" was the prime question.

"How bad is the working relationship between Mr Amoum and his boss, Mr Kiir?" The same question also applied to former Deputy Secretary-General, Dr Anne Ito.

Even more interestingly, both Amoum and Ito were nowhere to be found in Juba at that time.

All appearances to the contrary, this is not a finger pointing exercise. Not at all. I am trying to portray organizational dysfunction. A political party heading for campaigns and elections goes through internal processing.

Decisions are made where candidates for each post are identified as preferred or voted for internally. Thereby, the Party as an institution embarks on helping their candidates and prepares them with the necessary political and financial support.

Thusly, the candidates, in turn, begin campaigning for themselves on behalf of the party they belong to.

In the case of President Kiir, the SPLM presidential candidate in 2010, there was no programme. No staff or funds were allocated for his campaigns. In such a case, the two top SPLM General Secretariat staff were to be blamed or at least questioned.

It is worth noting here, two independent polling organizations including the USA-based NDI, National Democratic Institute, conducted opinion polls between 2008-2009 and found out that the SPLM's popularity was running at only 30%. Many were saying they would not vote for them. Ironically the same polls found that the most popular figure in Southern Sudanese politics was Mr Kiir. His popularity was at 98%. Could this have been the motive whereas the SPLM as a party did not organize a campaign programme for him?

Could it be that both Amoum and Ito were not interested in developing such a programme for their leader?

So many unanswered questions and time was not on our side.

Once informed of the problem, President Kiir formed a group of 12 members and called them his campaign team. This was led by his close associate, the late Dr Samson Kwaje. He was an SPLM political bureau member and the Southern Minister of Agriculture. I was also part of this team as the Presidential Candidate Communications Director.

I basically wrote his manifesto, political speeches, and organized all his media interviews. These included ones with

BBC's Hard Talk and CNN. The SPLM soft-spoken leader was a piece of work for me.

Every day at around 8 am, I had a session with him on how to speak in public.

On how to ensure to speak in full words, not acronyms and so forth. During the first three weeks of our campaign work, there was a huge transformation regarding Mr Kiir's public speaking abilities.

The other colleagues in the team also did their part. We had to work twenty days straight and travel to all the 10 states in the south. It simply 'had" to be done.

I wrote the manifesto and political travel schedule to 21 locations (counties, towns and villages) in 8 days, including campaign material. Through the logistics director, we were able to dispatch ourselves ahead of every mission to the destined location. We travelled by air, road, and even by foot to some remote locations.

We met hundreds of thousands of supporters. Campaign fever can be an amazing and unique experience. Media interviews were also 'really' interesting, especially if you are in a remote location with hardly any modern means of communication.

During the daytime, we were busy conducting political rallies in various locations. In the evening everyone ate dinner very hastily and began preparations for the next day. I retired to my laptop and worked on writing the daily media briefing for worldwide consumption.

I went to sleep at 3am and woke up by 5:30am daily. There was very limited time and unlimited work.

President Kiir easily won the election, carrying over ninety percent of the popular vote. Independent external monitors such as the Carter Centre, among others, verified it. Best of all, it went peacefully.

The Campaign Management Team (or CMT, as we called ourselves), congratulated ourselves on a job well done!

President Kiir was sworn into office during June of 2010. Then he swiftly formed his government. The Referendum was only a few months away.

Thereafter, I continued to work even more closely with him. He proposed that I take over the foreign affairs docket once Southern Sudan was free in 2011. He never fulfilled this promise. But that post was not my ambition. The referendum outcome and peace were my goals.

During September and October of 2010, a very alarming situation emerged. The United Nations was able to conduct their own independent "investigations" and found out that the Government had numerous corrupt officials. President Kiir was strongly advised to sack them all.

This became a critical issue given the referendum was so very close. Any cracks within the SPLM hierarchy would have far-reaching implications. Mr Kiir opted to turn a blind eye to these demands. Another sticky situation was brewing. The Government of Bashir decided to delay in the formation of the National Referendum Commission. By all intents and purposes, this should have taken place at the latest by August 2010. We were in trouble!

US President Barack Obama called for an emergency meeting of both President Kiir and Bashir's vice president Osman Taha. Bashir could not travel to the USA as he had, and still does have an ICC arrest warrant outstanding against him.

During this meeting, President Obama emphatically and

sternly directed both Sudanese leaders to expedite the formation of the national referendum commission. Any delays by any party would be sternly dealt with by America.

Immediately the two leaders returned to Sudan. The National Referendum Commission was formed in October 2010.

At last!

As for the national South Sudanese political parties, it was a different ball game altogether. They felt the SPLM dominated the political arena, and as such, they had very little space to reach out to the public. That was justified, and I personally sympathized with them. I tried my best to alert within the SPLM hierarchy that this was not politically healthy. However, reforming a liberation movement that turned into a political ruling party filled with thieves, was a task I certainly could not dream of overcoming.

I would not live for long being that naive!

So, I opted for quiet diplomacy. I conducted numerous meetings with Southern Sudanese political parties and took note of their grievances.

I used my close working relationship with Mr Kiir to convey these concerns to him and convinced him that if we did not play our cards right, we may jeopardize the referendum.

He was convinced and called for an all-South Sudanese political parties dialogue, November 2010. The delegates of these parties were able to openly air their concerns. The gaps were being bridged.

Once underway, the sessions went smoothly. Then surprisingly, President Kiir handed over the chair to his vice president, Dr Riek Machar. I was present and shocked by this.

Also at these meetings was Mr Amoum.

As a back-note: Constitutionally, political alliance work

between the SPLM and other political parties inside and outside Sudan was within my docket as foreign secretary. We had a rapporteur secretariat, which I supervised, and all evidence showed we were having successful sessions.

However, and very intriguingly, a Memorandum of Understanding was signed without the knowledge of the delegates, the SPLM Chairperson Mr Kiir or me!

To this day, I cannot claim who it was, because the secretariat had all the factual documentation. In no way whatsoever was there a provision to give other political parties 40% representation in the government post-referendum. In the 2010 general elections, the SPLM won by over 90%. So how on earth would political parties who garnered a fraction of the vote be given 40% of the seats?

I demanded to meet with Mr Kiir. I showed him the signed Memorandum of Understanding between the SPLM and the other political parties. It was signed by Mr Amoum.

President Kiir immediately called for an emergency all political parties meeting on the matter. He demanded to be told, who the engineers of the Memorandum were, and how was this 40% arrived at?

NO ONE ANSWERED.

Visibly angry, he presented two options. Either the country goes to snap general elections by December 2010 to settle it, or the SPLM grants the other political parties a reduction to 10% of the seats.

All delegates present agreed on the second option, citing that it was already November, and by December we must all begin working toward the January 2011 referendum.

A conspiracy was foiled!

But who was behind it and why? What was the 40% allocation all about? It remains a mystery to this day!

On January 13, 2011, all South Sudanese in Sudan and the Diaspora were lined up at IOM, International Organization of Movement centres worldwide. There they would register themselves and vote for their freedom. The long-anticipated Referendum was here. On February 14, the Sudan National Referendum Commission announced that the South Sudanese had voted for independence by over 98% in Sudan and worldwide! Jubilation, celebrations, and happiness were the order of the day. EVERYONE was happy. The United Nations endorsed this decision by a 99% vote of its membership. The world stood by South Sudan, and the future looked bright.

President Kiir swiftly appointed an ad-hoc constitutional reviewing committee to make a few amendments to the existing Interim Constitution. These would include such issues as the name of the republic, the national anthem, national army, foreign policy, and borders etc. All as per the norms of any sovereign country. Once again, due to a rather hurried draft, there was another mysterious clause in this constitution. I nabbed a copy (not being a member of the reviewing committee), and spent the whole night reading it word for word.

Something caught my eye.

The provision regarding the President and his tenure of office was highly dubious and cunning. It said in the case the president is rendered incapacitated etc., his Vice President immediately assumes office. Then, within a period of up to 6 months, the ruling Party (the SPLM) decides who will be the president until the next elections.

Knowing that President Kiir and his vice president Dr Riek Machar did not get along and that the ruling party was a mess,

I immediately sensed there could potentially be a very serious political power struggle if this clause was left as is.

I met with President Kiir, who again was clueless as to the contents of the document! Yes, the President was going to automatically ascent to the constitution while not knowing what the implications may be. Once I read out the relevant clause and showed him, he was stunned. He called his legal advisor and the clause was amended.

At this juncture, I began to question things regarding the constant political maneuverings, the President's capabilities, and that of those around him. It seemed like a tangled mess of schemes, ploys, and God knows what else. I was desperately hanging on for independence Then I would decide on what to do next with my career, and look out for my own safety.

I went back to work on my SPLM "Clean-Up" program and organized a small functional team within the secretariat. They were mostly on the ground in both Juba and Khartoum. I was always on the move: either meeting foreign diplomats, political parties, inside and outside Sudan, civil societies etc.

I had two passports: a diplomatic one, and a special passport (due to visa issues). At times I had to travel to several countries in a week. Obtaining visas was always an issue. Fortunately, the foreign embassies were always facilitating and equally keen to see if the SPLM would be capable of governing.

SPLM top brass was never at ease among themselves. Power positioning was the main issue.

It wasn't ethnic hate, or as has been portrayed, divisions among the people.

Rather it was ruling class greed. Of mastering the trick of 'divide and conquer'. Every one of them wanted to be both the

SPLM chairperson (constitutionally this would guarantee you the presidency), and the president. Seriously, the country's national interests never were the priority!

Finally, on the ninth of July 2011, we raised the flag!

World dignitaries, the media, and sympathizers of the South Sudanese cause poured into Juba. Tears flowed freely! It was beyond historic. It felt like everyone gained his or her own freedom that day. It was memorable!

We have arrived! Yet there was a tinge of sadness and foreboding.

Then all the hard work started. Some of us knew this; while others had no idea.

By end of 2011 political matters increasingly became bitter between the Republic of South Sudan and its former "mother" country Sudan. Khartoum started playing dirty tricks regarding oil revenue. South Sudan is landlocked and has no port or oil handling infrastructure. Khartoum was (and still is) the only gateway for 90% of the country's income.

President Kiir lost his cool and shut down oil exploration. The new country began an abrupt journey of economic hardships. However, via diplomatic efforts and dialogue, oil flow resumed, and matters seemed to settle. But corruption was rampant and President Kiir remained silent on the matter.

By March 2012, and in a rather surprising move, Mr Kiir wrote individual letters to about 75 senior government officials accusing them of theft of up to $4 billion and corruption. He requested that they return the stolen money into an account he opened in Kenya.

Not surprisingly, no one acted, and it was business as usual. Mr Kiir did not commence any further follow-up action.

THE SALVA KIIR YEARS

The risen hopes of millions of South Sudanese were thereby shattered.

That is when I believe he began losing credibility regarding his ability to lead South Sudan and to clean up the corruption.

However, once more and in another surprise move, in January 2013, he decided to retire about 150 senior army officers, including generals. The SPLA had more generals than the American army.

This was perhaps, the best decision he had made since 2005. Those officers had bullied the country. They should have been retired at least 20 years earlier. They were dead weight on the public purse. The entourage of military personnel assigned to them was a huge additional cost as well.

In any case, some of us thought this would pave the way for reforms. Hopefully, training of a more professional and younger national army could begin. Three months later, the President fired two senior ministers on corruption charges. Next, in July, he fired the entire cabinet on corruption and incompetence charges. Even my former boss, Mr Amoum, was put under investigation regarding mismanagement of funds. I was elated and met with the President, congratulating him on his decisions. I advised him to swiftly appoint competent professional patriotic South Sudanese to deliver badly needed services. I thought that he listened.

A couple months passed. President Kiir, being himself, collected a... well I really don't know how to describe such a 'stranger than fiction' cabinet team. With the exception of one or two passably competent individuals, it was a mess. Honestly, the team he swore in as his cabinet was a group of individuals lacking vision, plans, or programmes. They had no idea of how to run a ministry. They had no desire learn their roles! This was the start of the demise of a potentially great nation.

However, the President may have underestimated the consequences of his decisions. He missed a very important factor. He hadn't assembled regional and international support for his moves.

I suppose, his military background had conditioned him to make decisions in complete secrecy and without consultation. Consensus building prior support for his decisions was unknown to him.

He did not discuss any of these decisions with anyone including with myself.

Despite the fact his measures were most welcomed nationally, those removed from the government were a few steps ahead of him. They had developed very strong international relationships, and presented themselves as being viable alternatives leaders to Kiir.

They included Dr Machar, Mama Rebecca Nyandeng (wife of the late Dr Garang), Mr Amoum, Deng Alor, and others.

This same group, although they were foes in the past, networked nationally and made plans to consolidate their agenda for a change of regime.

There were questions begging answers. Did President Kiir and his security apparatus know of all this? If so, why did they not plan their own strategies to woo the regional and the world community? I think the President was not aware of how advanced his former colleagues were regarding their planning. He assumed that by being the President, he could fire them, and that would be the end of the story.

Near the end of 2013, President Kiir was away on an official mission to France. He then proceeded on to attend Nelson

Mandela's funeral in South Africa. The SPLM figures who had fallen out with Kiir, became one entity.

'Historical figures' or 'a disgruntled group' was how they were portrayed in the media. They began meeting regularly and discussed ways to oust Mr Kiir from the SPLM Chairmanship, and consequently from the presidency. But this could not happen without the proper Party mechanisms being activated and followed.

Upon the return of the President from his overseas obligations, the SPLM called for an emergency National Liberation Council meeting for the 13th to 15th of December 2013 in Juba. I was there, as were about 150 other delegates. From the body language, one would easily observe there were sharp divisions between Mr Kiir and the plotters. Tension was rife throughout.

None of them, including the President, would talk about these issues.

We waited, and listened to a few delegates presenting random issues. It was surreal.

On the second day, the 'disgruntled' ones did not attend. They boycotted the meeting and had already announced to the *Sudan Tribune* that the atmosphere was not conducive for them to participate.

By Sunday 15th December 2013, the meetings were over. As we all headed home, gunfire was heard all over Juba. It started in the meeting venue, the Nyakuren Cultural Centre, and spread very quickly to the rest of the city.

We all had to run to home for cover. Juba became very unsafe, very quickly. Nobody slept that night.

Around 1pm, Monday 16th December 2013, the President, flanked by his Ministers of Defense, Mr Kuol Manyang, Interior, Mr Aleu Aleu and Foreign Affairs, Mr Benjamin Marial, announced that there was a failed military coup during the night by vice-president Dr Riek Machar and others. He further stated that the government was fully in control of the situation and pursuing the culprits.

The following day, all of them were arrested except Dr Machar and his wife Mama Angelina Teny. They seemed to have fled the country. The arrested group were later known as Former Detainees, FDs/Group 10.

More famously, they were known as "the Garang Boys". These were top SPLM operatives who were very close to Dr Garang. They were rumoured to have enjoyed many privileges over the years. It was felt that they had become untouchable.

Eventually, and with mediation and guarantees by Kenya's President Uhuru Kenyatta, these FDs were bailed out and freed.

By its close, 2013 was sour and tragic. A complete opposite of its beautiful beginning!

The new year ushered in a long stretch of a senseless war. Peace negotiations facilitated by the Intergovernmental Authority of Development, IGAD finally resulted in the brokering of a deal in September 2015.

Giving and sharing power, plus the usual political appeasements crept back into government. Never mind the bloodshed, the suffering, and the pain experienced by the people.

The politicians had agreed, or so it seemed. Finally, by April, the ousted leaders started arriving in Juba to reclaim their former posts. It would be business as per usual. The poor, suffering, population simply had no choice but to accept it. If appeasing politicians, and giving them powerful posts would bring peace, so be it.

However, the agreement barely lasted a couple of months. Then, another violent drama unfolded. Dr Machar and his long-term foe President Kiir fought inside the Presidential Palace. Once more, heavy gunfire was heard all over the capital. It was especially rampant in the Palace.

Once more, Dr Machar and his wife fled the country. Mr Taban Deng and his colleagues from Riek Machar's group known as SPLM In-Opposition, IO opted to remain with Kiir. Together, they formed an alliance and a coalition government. This remains intact at the time of writing. However, peace was far from being attained.

I deliberately do not want to delve into more details on whether there was a failed military coup or a staged, false military coup. This is simply because, to this day, I do not know.

There seems to have been an earlier detailed plan to start a rebellion by Machar. His group and the "White Army", were able to sustain a senseless war for more than two years in different parts of the greater Upper Nile and some parts of Equatoria. In order to run a war for that length of time, a great deal of prior logistics and planning was required.

Even more tragically, South Sudan was never the same. Thousands of innocents were killed regardless of their ethnicities.

Nuer, Dinka, Chollo and other minorities in Bahr al Ghazal and some from Equatoria. Many others were slaughtered as well. These were people caught up in the senseless war of those who either want power desperately or by those who want to hang on to power equally desperately. These selfish leaders simply do not care for the lives of the innocent ones. Neither do they care for the hundreds of thousands internally displaced persons, raped women, dying children, and millions of other refugees who fled to the nearest borders. The ailing, failing, economy is another shame. The leadership of the country has lost direction, or rather never had any to begin with.

Between 2014 and October 2016, I desperately tried to lay out scenarios to President Kiir. I spent countless hours detailing plans that I sincerely had hoped would help rescue the Country. They ranged from trust-building to national dialogue, to amnesty for all, to ending appeasement of criminals in government, to firing all incompetent thieves, to grassroots people on people, peace dialogues.

I pushed him regarding opening up South Sudan for its Diaspora to return so they could help build, and also bridge the ethnic hate. I asked him to utilize women's roles in peacemaking, and that he needed to build strong foreign relation ties. That he must reach out to sincere advice from any well-wishers.

President Kiir always listened very attentively to me, or so I thought. But he never implemented any of our 'agreed' plans.

October 25th, 2016, was my very last face-face meeting with President Kiir. I tried one last time to convince him to save the country from collapsing and disintegrating.

His reaction? It did not matter anymore. He did not say that *per se*, but his body language said as much.

Both Dr Riek Machar and President Kiir know too well how to divide and rule for their own selfish gains.

They pitted the Dinka and Nuer against each other for no other reason than to access, or remain in power!

How could a founding president of a country such as South Sudan, which was burdened historically with slavery, discriminatory policies, death, famine, political starvation, second-class citizenry, displacement, refuge, rape, mass killings, ethnic cleansing, and suffering that no amount of words can be ever adequate to describe, allow such atrocities to continue?

How could the founding president of a people whose hopes

and dreams were only to be free and live as dignified people, decide to abandon them and watch them suffer under his watch without doing a thing?

How could a president of the world's newest nation not humble himself and say, "I have failed to serve you. Please let's call for elections so you may choose your own leader who may serve you better than myself."

So, this was how it was with President Kiir. I believed in his leadership and worked faithfully for him for over seven years. I looked out for him for the sake of our country and our people. But after all that, I have finally realized that the ruling class of South Sudan, headed by President Kiir, was no different from any of the armed rebellion leaders.

The list of those who failed us is extensive. Beginning with President Kiir. Dr Riek Machar, Wani Igga, Pagan Amoum, Deng Alor, Mama Rebecca Nyandeng, Taban Deng, and many more.

THEY ALL FAILED US!

I am equally ready to be publicly audited for any failure on my part during my tenure as SPLM foreign secretary, and my commitment years to peace for South Sudan for 18 years.

THE PEOPLE OF SOUTH SUDAN DESERVE A PUBLIC HEARING, AND ACCOUNTABILITY, TO LEARN ABOUT AND KNOW ALL THOSE WHO WRONGED THEM.

What happened in South Sudan should not be left unanswered.

The pain, ethnic hate and divisions among the people, and the loss of lives and generations ARE important. We have a right to know who did what and why! JUSTICE should be a fundamental pillar in the nation-building of the state. The country is more divided than it was during the two civil wars. We now have seventeen armed groups operating in the area.

There is more ethnic hate and killings than ever experienced in the history of South Sudan.

Poverty is beyond description. It is lucky if one gets a meal once every three days! There are no medicines. No medical help.

Under President Kiir, the Nuer were ethnically killed in Juba in December 2013. In reaction, under Dr Riek Machar the country was ethnically polarized during the 2013-2015 war of Nuer vs Dinka. His "White Army" focused on ethnically cleansing the Dinka in Bor, Malakal, Bentiu and Renk.

Kiir, on the other hand, continues to favour his own relatives, cousins, nephews and in-laws over other qualified competent South Sudanese.

Many South Sudanese intellectuals and politicians, even among the Diaspora, also have begun aligning themselves alongside tribal lines.

Tragically, due to Kiir's nepotism regarding his own clan (which is a subsection of the Dinka community, but by no means represents all Dinka), many Dinka today are victims of hate by other ethnic communities in South Sudan.

The entire house of cards is falling down!

The SPLM

"When united: SPLM luminaries are stealing."
"When divided: SPLM luminaries are fighting while stealing."
This is the mantra of the South Sudanese today.

The SPLM worked selflessly for over 20 years, with thousands of foot soldiers and freedom fighters. They gave their lives and souls to free the oppressed.

Remaining behind were hundreds of thousands of widows, orphans, and the physically challenged. There were many other sacrifices the South Sudanese gave voluntarily to free themselves.

All this meant nothing to the SPLM ruling class. They feigned amnesia while turning blind eyes and deaf ears to the liberation struggle legacy.

Before the ink dried on the CPA, SPLM luminaries turned against their promises of liberation, justice, liberty, and equality.

Between 2005 and 2011 the ruling class of the SPLM became the 'everything' that ran the regional government. Financial and freedoms policing were totally under their control.

A far cry from liberation.

To this day, no one knows how this poisonous governance by the SPLM started. Was it there since its inception in 1983-2005 during its bush war days? Or did it surface after attaining peace? Who are the exact culprits?

Too many questions without answers I suppose.

One notable factor is that the same power clique of 1983 were still there in 2005. My first inclination would be to start there when looking for corruption! Some of us overlooked this creeping 'disease' in order to focus on the bigger picture.

Most notably that would be during the 6-year interim period.

It was imperative that the South Sudanese must have their long-awaited referendum to decide their destiny, at any cost.

If, for example, NESI or someone like myself would have opted to openly discuss government corruption during those years, it would have opened a Pandora's box of woe. It may have put to risk the referendum and the CPA itself.

That calamity could have shuttered the more than half-century quest to be free at last. The world community focus would have most likely been lost. South Sudan might slide back into a civil war worse than any seen there before.

I interviewed many ordinary people, men and women alike, about the possibility of not conducting the referendum. Their answer was: "This time even the old folks would fight! Everyone would fight!"

Such emphatic statements scared me. I decided together with my NESI partners that peace was better than war any time.

We decided to keep corruption a low key priority and give the South Sudanese a clear road to the referendum. If there was any time people counted years and wished them to be months or

THE SPLM

days, it was us. Yes, we wanted the time to fly. We couldn't wait for the referendum to be conducted and the real fight for justice, anti-corruption, and liberties to begin upon the declaration of independence!

I realized that there was a clear disconnection between SPLM as an organization with certain principles, and the SPLM hierarchy/leadership understanding and adhering to these principles!

As a result of this disconnection, the SPLM let the people of Southern Sudan down. Shattered dreams and the aspirations of more than 40 years of fighting. Gone! So many were wounded or lost their lives. Much more were displaced as refugees. Property loss was staggering. We can only weep for those generations that hung on in noble hope. Those that survived felt totally hopeless, helpless, and betrayed.

Tragic and undeserved!

The SPLM hierarchy became increasingly consumed with looting the public purse. Dubious contracts worth hundreds of millions of dollars were handed out like candy (provided the requisite kickbacks were paid). The people's money purchased expensive mansions and apartments. The new ruling class filled car showrooms and expensive shops. Limited edition neck ties and solid gold cell-phones became their obsession.

My prime point was that by that time, the SPLM had almost vanished from the political scene. We were taking the risk that the peace agreement, might be thrown in the trash.

The SPLM was not ready to be both the ruling party and the liberating party. It operated as a guerrilla movement with impeccable rules, regulations, and vision, but no actual implementation of any of it.

Furthermore, the SPLM failed to organize and restructure itself.

It failed to transform itself from a movement to a political party, let alone a ruling party. A few powerful individuals ran both the SPLM and the government. To them, that was what it meant to be a political party. By granting themselves dubious contracts and rewarding themselves anything from the national budget. This thievery translated itself to them, that they were the ruling party.

Individuals substituted for organization. This did and continues to negatively impact governance and systems establishment. When powerful individuals parade around as if they are governmental and organizational institutions, the country has little to no hope. It could never ever build itself into a functioning state. Some of us tried to address and highlight these issues within the SPLM. I even went as far as establishing a fully functional foreign docket. But my senior colleagues refused, or could not comprehend, the need for workable policies, systems, and organizations of establishment. It simply became a no-go zone. I felt extremely isolated.

However, I did not let up!

We had about one year to go, and our country would be free. So, I focused on what I 'could' do. I tried my best to overlook all the other messes around me.

The SPLM, even as dysfunctional as they were, had the advantage over all other political parties. This was simply because, for over 20 years during the bush war, most of the population knew of them. In fact, the SPLM has always been referred to as "hakuma" (government in Arabic). Even after signing the CPA in 2005, they continued to enjoy the same status; albeit with decreasing popularity from the people. All due to corrupt and just plain stupid practises. However, the SPLM still maintained that added advantage.

THE SPLM

The South Sudanese believed: "Better the devil you know than the angel you don't know."

There are many unresolved issues within the SPLM hierarchy.

As an organization, it seems to have had its flaws since its inception. I will not delve much into the very early years, as am not an authority on that matter.

However, as a body it has suffered organizational, methodological, and systematic disorders, that led to the SPLM of today. I will elaborate.

The SPLM from the outset in 1983 appears to have been a "one-man" show, revolving around the late Dr Garang. When I joined in 1998, many older and senior SPLM cadres warned me that soon I would be subjected to unquestionable orders from him. They said the SPLM was not an organization I could influence or reform.

I was given several examples of how he (and his wife) ran the SPLM as their own personal fiefdom. Anyone who opposed either of them would eventually pay the price, including your life. I listened, and I kept doing my work participating in the peace negotiations. I tried my best not to agitate.

Although I have always been a reformist, I focused on the 'bigger picture'. The goal was to attain a just and lasting peace that embodied human rights, women's rights, and equality.

To me, stopping the bloodshed was my utmost priority. I was barely 24 then, and perhaps I did not fully comprehend that ideals and ideology are often the first victims of power.

That if an organization "preaches" justice and equality, it must itself practice these values. It was only a matter of time before the SPLM, as an organization, would one day begin to show the damaging cracks.

There was no culture of questioning the wrongs of top SPLM members. The bad governance practices such as favouritism, nepotism, tribalism, dictatorship, and non-transparency, are some of the many traits that became entrenched in the SPLM over the years.

In the 1980s, those who tried to question these governance ills either were punished by being sent into SPLM jails for years or simply "mysteriously" perished. By the 1990s, questions were asked, and the SPLM conformed to what the commander-in-chief, Dr Garang said, or decided with his close associates. Like most other South Sudanese, young/upcoming ones like myself remained somewhat clueless. However, most older reformists and intellectuals opted to peacefully tag along. They hoped one day the time would come to address the rot within the SPLM once peace was achieved. In retrospect, that was a poor choice.

Along with wanting to spend time with my son, this is perhaps an underlying reason I later decided to opt out of the government role offered to me by Dr Garang.

The SPLM was the only system Southern Sudan knew, and thus resembled the only governance system. Sadly, this set an extremely damaging precedent regarding the foundation of the world's youngest nation.

Bad governance became the face of the SPLM. Senior SPLM luminaries felt no shame when abusing his or her powerful position to steal millions in public funds. It was not shameful to appoint your incompetent relatives into any government/public post. There was no sin in awarding your relatives government-sponsored scholarships while sidelining much more competent and deserving South Sudanese.

The gap between the ruling class and the masses grew wider and wider every single day. Knowledge of dubious contracts was

THE SPLM

openly discussed everywhere in major cities like Juba, Wau, or Malakal.

These informal gatherings were called "the local parliaments".

Political discussions became the daily routine for non-politicians. The population became highly aware of all the wrongs in the country.

One wonders why the population did not reach a boiling point and rise against the system. Perhaps their dream of freedom kept them patient, and in check.

Meanwhile, the SPLM-led government continued to loot unashamedly. Political party appointees in senior posts copied the practice. They too looted and subsequently appointed their own relatives and friends. The 6-year CPA interim period became a particularly bleak and shameful period in the history of the country to be. People decided to turn a blind eye to all government wrongs and clung unto one hope. In July 2011 they would gain their independence.

For individuals like myself who joined the system, it was far too late to rescue anything from a corrupt sinking ship.

I had tried my utmost to convince the world, via my role, that there could be hope towards uprooting bad governance. After all, the South was not yet a country. I also tried my best to advise South Sudan leader, President Kiir. I hoped he would begin compiling evidence of corruption to address the culprits once our independence was gained. We all continued to work in the hope that all these wrongs could be undone once freedom was attained.

However, as any group of individuals who enjoy the perks of power either monetarily or via influence, they had their own plans on how to continue to loot and rule us 'forever'.

The reformists were hoping and working hard on building like-minded alliances. They were formulating plans for post-Independence South Sudan. The looters began building their own network nationally, regionally, and internationally so they could retain power. They wanted to fully control the world's newest nation's vast natural riches.

It was (and is) a tragedy of epic proportions.

The SPLM luminaries selfish, non-visionary agenda would be consolidated during the 6-year interim period. They ensured that they had their own like-minded corrupt, incompetent, tribalist individuals placed in government, embassies, the national army, the legislature (the national and states parliaments were not spared), the executive, and the judiciary.

Even the private sector was infiltrated! There were no checks or balances in place from the onset of the peace agreement through to independence.

As I closely monitored these schemes, I realized that my chances of surviving alive grew thinner and thinner. I had to lie very, very low if I were to continue serving in my role. I was the "invisible" foreign secretary. My closest associates were the only ones who knew where I lived in Juba. I kept several telephone numbers and I spent each night in a different hotel or a relative's home to disguise my whereabouts.

Death was a reality.

I knew who these powerful people were. Each day, I knew more regarding the level of their associations and some of their plans as well. They knew I knew. Mr Amoum, for instance, made sure I was never granted any budget to implement our annual foreign

THE SPLM

projections. I did not even have the funds to make international calls or use the internet. He blocked my work with all means at his disposal.

To add salt to my wounds, he ordered the finance department not to give me any medical or housing allowance. My salary was far lower than all other secretaries. I realized all this was done to frustrate me, so I would quit. I had to sell personal and family property to make ends meet between 2008-2015. I took out bank loans and depleted personal savings. I could barely manage to do my work, let alone take care of my child. But my will was not broken. I continued.

Then, my security became an issue. A very serious one! It was mid-2012. Almost every night without fail, someone would come very close to where I lived and would shoot in the air. I slept under my bed almost every night as a result. My younger brother Jambo Jr. lived with me and witnessed it all.

It was a very frightening experience that went on for at least six months. I reported the matter to the President, who in turn (and in a rather aloof manner) told me not to fear anything. That the shooter was only trying to scare me. I requested a security detail. He declined, claiming there was no need.

I also spoke with the President regarding the disparity of budget and remuneration between myself and others at my level. He calmly assured me that soon the SPLM would be audited and wrongs shall be addressed.

In the end, I simply persisted despite the daily ordeal of shootings. The SPLM was, a time bomb waiting to explode due to the lack of any real organization. There was no implementation of rules and regulations. A few powerful individuals ran the show. It was not an evolving democratic organization. Its hierarchy since inception remained the same aside from those who died like Garang. It has always been an exclusive club, gorging on self-entitlement and money.

It was a far cry from the romantic notion of a liberation movement that evolves and moves with its membership. There was no plan in place to mentor and groom new leadership candidates under rules and regulations respected by all.

For instance, the only times the SPLM would hold organizational meetings as the national liberation council would be on reactive grounds. Never as per the SPLM constitution and norms. The membership was left completely out of the loop when it came time to deliberate on important matters and burning issues.

SPLM's stated rules and values never made the transition from a liberation movement into a political party. As the ruling party, its stated principles were not applied as government policies.

The membership had too many unanswered questions and was lacking the constitutional forums to discuss them. As well, the SPLM's Seventh Front (the Diaspora) historically, and during the struggle, were at the forefront lobbying the world about the South Sudanese (and other marginalized communities) issues. Reaching out to the public in their host countries, they sought out policymakers such as Senators, Congresspersons, Parliamentarians, and civil society.

Then, the SPLM Diaspora suddenly was completely left out of decision making for the mostly illiterate nation to be. I tried my utmost to lobby within the SPLM ranks in Juba to have the Diaspora channelled officially to be part of nation-building. They were a critical factor given their badly needed education and expertise. All this fell on deaf ears.

THE SPLM

A similar refrain to the old and well-worn revolutionary edict: "As soon as the Revolution is won, kill the intellectuals!" Intellectuals, being what they are... intellectual, don't recognise genocidal types like Stalin and Mao, for being what they 'are'. The revolution gets a lot less fun when you are the one being marginalised, or simply deleted from the equation.

Today, there are numerous armed groups in the country. Increasingly, more stalwarts defect from Kiir's government. The most recent at the time of writing being a veteran loyalist General from Equatoria, Mr Thomas Cirillo Swaka.

Citing tribalism and corruption as reasons for his defection, he formed his own armed movement.

An Equatorian who defected earlier in 2015, was the former governor of Western Equatoria State, Mr Joseph Bakosoro, cited bad governance.

Basically, once a peace agreement is signed, another avenue for war is opened. The mistakes and loopholes in these peace agreements, run along the following lines: These are not peace agreements. Rather they are political agreements made to temporarily appease.

The root causes of these conflicts are never discussed openly and transparently. Neither are the so-called peace talks inclusive and consultative.

The people of South Sudan have never been part of any of these talks. No leader or politician can take up arms without the support of his or her aggrieved community. It would make perfectly logical sense that these communities are included, consulted with, and their grievances are addressed when truly trying to bring about a just agreement.

Grassroots peace talks have been completely lacking from the political vision in South Sudan. Certainly, a country hit by decades of civil conflicts is highly traumatized and bruised. Generations are born to nothing but war and violence. There needs to be a more holistic approach. This may take many years and long-term resources. Far less cost, however, than that used in armed conflict. Can there really be a price put on stopping bloodshed?

Unless the SPLM owns up to its mistakes and goes back to the drawing board; unrest will become a revolution.

Unless the SPLM admits its gross violations against the people of South Sudan and makes genuine attempts to redeem its legacy of having organized and liberated South Sudan, it shall go down in history as the liberation movement that failed to live up to its vision and values. The one that failed to salvage itself, thereby sinking the country.

That would be the most shameful fall: From Grace to Grass!

It seems the more senior you are in SPLM, the more you enjoy subjecting juniors to all manner of violations. Yes, to a significant extent it became another form of oppression and harassment. This was akin to the stories of hazing and abuse in British 'public' schools. Juniors had to follow 'all' orders from seniors. Wrong or right, it did not matter. This is when I also began to realize that militarized organizations, in the long run, cannot be the solution. If liberation is achieved, the old boss is simply replaced by the new boss.

They have the same mentality. They are rulers. Citizens are mere subjects or cattle!

I kept asking myself what other choices did I have really? I am all alone. Kiir's government would never listen to a peaceful non-entity like me. As for the SPLM, maybe I could contribute toward reforming it.

THE SPLM

But that was not my main goal. The realist in me saw that the majority of the leadership was too rigid to listen to talk of reforms and transformation. So, I resigned myself to contribute in order to free the South Sudanese.

Today, however, I have finally 'seen the light'. I realize that the SPLM is a parasite. It has refused to reform itself. It has failed the Republic of South Sudan. It has failed to meet the visions and ideals of the people.

It is a failure! It should be no more!

The Diaspora

When it became the ruling party, the SPLM hierarchy and luminaires quietly forgot about all the Diaspora aid it had received. This led to disappointment, fragmentation, demoralization, and anger among those out of the country.

Once I took up the foreign relations docket of the SPLM, I reached out to many of our still active Diaspora. They were so eager to hear from Juba!

For once they felt someone noticed them, and that was very moving. In a short while, I was able to develop some questionnaires, so I could understand their structural and organizational dynamics.

Every country was different, and I had to bear this in mind while developing the first SPLM Diaspora Guidelines. We worked tirelessly with the volunteer chapters and ad-hoc leaders. Together, we were able to help introduce the framework which led to elections and optimized organizational abilities.

I will always appreciate the selfless commitment and patriotism of Kenneth Elisapana, Regina of Norway, Dr Johnson Mogga, Mangok Mayen, Bella Kodi, Gisma Mou Mou, Daniel Ater,

THE DIASPORA

Santino Fardol, Martin Muortat, Santino Atem Deng, and many more.

Organizing was extremely useful and instrumental. It was anticipated the South Sudanese Diaspora would vote in both the 2010 General Elections and the 2011 Referendum. As a result, and without political bias, they helped organize the almost one million South Sudanese in North America, Australia, Europe, Egypt, Eastern, and Southern Africa.

Time zones had no effect on our constant email communications.

It is worth noting that I worked closely with the regional Government of Southern Sudan, GoSS on: Alerting GoSS of the Diaspora zones (countries where they are present).

It was crucial regarding its negotiations with the UN IOM, International Organization of Movement. The IOM was mandated with allocating adequate Diaspora voter's registration centres worldwide. Given the long distances and vast countries, each apparatus was set up beforehand.

Those host countries, especially in Europe, needed to facilitate fast-track visas for our far-flung people. Many did not have residence permits in their host countries. The IOM Centre for Europe was only in the United Kingdom, but the Diaspora lived throughout. Under current regulations, they would have had to travel to the UK.

They had no guarantee that they could return. The UK Government was very instrumental in understanding this serious concern and arranged that all South Sudanese would have identity cards available to them. They could then simply go to the nearest UK embassy, where they were granted a visa. In addition, the UK government waivered visa fees.

FANTASTIC! We shall always be grateful to the IOM, and the United Kingdom in particular, for this facilitation. The Diaspora in Europe were able to vote! They could help shape our destiny!

Looking at the bigger picture, politically, I was also able to convince President Kiir, also the SPLM Chairperson, at a meeting in October 2010. This was crucial to harmonize relations with other Southern political parties and have one common goal.

We needed to be united, to gain trust.

I am most grateful to these political parties for deciding to choose South Sudan's destiny as their priority, over their well-deserved grievances with the SPLM.

I remained optimistic that the Government of the Republic of South Sudan would work to implement, to the letter, the "state of the art" SPLM foreign policy I helped draft in September 2009. I believe it would be a win-win policy for South Sudan and the world. As well, the government ought to have worked closely with its vast Diaspora.

They have the education, expertise, connections, and skills that could help transform a semi-literate nation into a driving force within Africa.

Perhaps even the world. We need their help to build a nation based on vision, equality, justice, and prosperity.

In all honesty, what will likely transpire over time is what has happened with every other far-flung, displaced people. The struggle to remain relevant, and connected, is not favoured by history. Ask any second or third generation immigrant who their relatives are in the 'old' country, and they will have to think hard about the question. Old Cubanistas in Florida shake their fists at Castro; to no avail.

THE DIASPORA

If the Diaspora is to be effective, it must act sooner than later. Its children will favour the home they know. Just as mine does.

Africa's Brain Drain

At the micro level within the SPLM, you are in a rigid system. It is filled by egoistic, militarized, and outdated individuals. They are rigidly traditionalist in their way of life and thinking.

However, this movement had a noble vision and mission. The SPLM has this huge potential to achieve its unique set of ideals. This holds true not only in South Sudan but possibly the entire continent.

At the macro level, Africa has yet to begin to realize its potential. Decades after colonial rule, dysfunction and greed seem to be the norm.

Africa needs a genuine revolution. One by, with, and for the people.

It is ironic that what may be the world's naturally richest continent is the poorest one regarding its inhabitants. There is no logical explanation whatsoever to this retarded reality in Africa today! Civil wars, dictatorships, rewarding incompetence, criminals, corrupt government and private sector officials. Hunger, disease, ethnic hate, tribalism. The same failed ruling class recycling itself endlessly.

AFRICA'S BRAIN DRAIN

The exclusive, so-called 'African Union Club' of Presidents are the root cause of many of Africa's tragedies.

How do liberation ideals and genuine reformists survive in such paradigm sets? Selfish greedy rulers block Africa's never-ending and yet hopeless desire of becoming stable and progressive.

It saddens me to admit that many educated and skilled Africans often decide to opt out. Instead, they offer their services to the Western world and other countries. These elite professionals often feel sidelined and under-appreciated in their home continent.

They find it hard to work in the extremely corrupt incompetent, non-professional atmosphere of African society.

It is quite painful for me, as an African optimist and reformist, to see them leave. I acknowledge the hurt in myself over this, but I also sympathize with our African professional Diaspora.

They choose to seek greener pastures overseas. Even the most patriotic and resilient African professional faces that time, when he or she decides that they have had enough of Africa. Enough of corrupt political leaders cavorting in bed with the corrupt private sector. Enough of witnessing the rape of Africa's potential. The looting of her riches. Mismanaging her to death.

Adding insult to injury, those that pillage are so extremely greed driven, they leave not even a crumb for their fellow Africans. Citizens in oil-rich countries such as Nigeria, Angola, South Sudan, DR Congo and others, easily go for days without fuel, food, or electricity!

What a travesty!

You have countries in Africa with vast reserves of oil, gold, and diamonds. Others with water and fertile land. Yet their people cannot feed themselves. They cannot provide an education for their children.

Often these countries are hit by micro-conflicts throughout the land. They lead to hunger, displacement, and death. South Sudan, DR Congo, Sierra Leone and Libya are classic examples.

On the surface, the reasons for such chronic conflicts appear to be power wrangling between influential individuals and religion. Ones who would do anything to either remain in power or ascend to power.

However, the real underpinning issues that prolong these conflicts, seems to be their earnest desire to control the vast natural resources. Often, they are partnered with dodgy international partners, including multinationals and governments.

How will Africa ever get out of this mess? Can it?

The same elite ruling class continues to exert its will in most African countries. Do we need to rise and revolt peacefully against them, or do we simply try to leave? Are the answers that black and white?

I can tell you clearly, armed revolutions do not work for peoples that want to be free. They will not achieve the liberation or the emancipation of Africa. All that is achieved is a culture of violence and the creation of more corrupt dictatorial regimes. The bloodshed, mass destruction, lawlessness and violence negatively influence the young. They grow up knowing nothing but how to square grievances violently. Violence breeds violence!

In my opinion, the best solution for Africa is civic awareness. Mass constitutional education in our curriculum system. Social gatherings, at universities, etc.

Think-tanks are useful. The formation of groups of average people, professional groups, and others. They must take it upon themselves to work towards a solution. The way to ending Africa's bad governance lies in our collective unrelenting peaceful efforts!

Eventually, Africa's population will begin to act and feel like citizens, not subjects. They must ensure to only elect competent leaders.

Ones who must be servants of their constituencies. They must be checked and balanced constitutionally.

Constitutionalism in Africa must become the order of the day, and our way of life. It must be so if Africa is to rise and realize her full potential.

The African diaspora must also be part of this reform and transformation processes. "You can run, but you can't hide!" Africa will always be home at the end of the day!

Children of Freedom Fighters

I wonder about the children of freedom fighters. What effect does living without their fathers have on them?

Often wars are led and fought by men. They are the ones who take up arms and hence end up being absent from their children's lives. Women end up assuming the role of father and mother. Parenting should involve both. The absence of the father is most painfully felt.

South Sudan has many generations born during its two main civil wars. Tragically, millions of children were raised just by their mothers. The fathers were either fighting or killed.

Other countries and world bodies have researched this type of situation. I strongly believe this an area that needs to be looked at deeply from a South Sudanese point of view.

We need to know how much such an upbringing has impacted on these children born during conflicts and wars, displacement, and refugee status. All these factors are bound to negatively affect any human being.

Perhaps, this partially explains as well, the "nature of violence" and the vicious cycle of conflict in today's South Sudan. I am not an expert on such a topic; on human behaviour regarding this form of violence. However, using common sense and personal observations, I am almost certain there is a direct link between prolonged conflicts and the nature of people's behaviour. Did their childhood leave them missing 'something' that fuels a need for violence?

Even in conventional stable societies, absent fathers or mothers (or both) from their children's lives, remains a key psychological and social issue for debate regarding their well-being and upbringing.

Children brought up in single-parent homes remain an issue of continuous research and debate. The stigma remains within them, and the scars are there.

Psychologically, we have no idea how much damage the imbalance of gender care has wrought. But it is most certainly a problem!

One wonders where would one begin with these children?

Some of those children born between 1955 and 1972 are now great-grandparents.

Similarly, this also applies to the war of 1983-2005. So many of the children born during this period are parents. These generations born into war, who saw and experienced violence, are perhaps the ones who may finally bring about justice and closure.

Democratic and peaceful means of action are seldom even conceptualized by most South Sudanese born during the conflicts.

We all have some things to think about:

- Do any of the generations who missed out on their fathers being around, honestly comprehend the meaning of a nuclear family comprising both parents? I wonder. Are the psychological effects permanent, or is there a way to help people work through them?
- Could this explain why the citizens of a country such as South Sudan, with its prolonged wars, finds it hard to conceive peaceful democratic means as a way of rule?
- What will be the future of such a country be? How long will it have to endure this plague?
- How much support, other than the "conventional" means often given by regional and international governments, needs to be extended to such a country? I believe these should include trauma counselling, socio-cultural understanding, and perhaps political processes need to be influenced by such psychological support mechanisms.

I have come to realize that if in a conventional stable "civil" society there are many challenges regarding parenting, then there is an even greater need in South Sudan. There are layers upon layers of complex, socio-psychological, and behavioural challenges of a very serious nature. The lost generations born during South Sudan's civil wars need to be found again! They are truly in dire need to be examined and communally and openly discussed as part of stabilizing the country, and as a way to realizing lasting peace.

Many psychologists believe that one must make peace within themselves before making peace with the community, and society as a whole. Obviously, there are many unresolved inner issues among millions of South Sudanese. It goes all the way to the top. This must be addressed fully.

On the other hand, we have another serious case. The children born outside of South Sudan. Refugees and others whose parents fled over the years. Many of them acquired citizenship in the host countries. Their education and lifestyle is both different and distinct from that of the native South Sudanese.

The Diaspora families live on the surface peacefully with a conventional lifestyle. However, many long to be home. They're torn between worlds. But home is not at peace. There are few basic social services such as education and health for their children in South Sudan. Their children are a disproportionate percentage of the criminal element in their new countries.

However, in my work with these Diaspora, I have felt their pain. It is particularly apparent in the adults. They have an extreme yearning to return. They are not peace within themselves. They wish to ensure their kids receive a good education, live in a peaceful environment and enjoy the other amenities offered where they live now. But, they also wish their children could be in the homeland, and enjoy living their culture and with their people. It's a trapped feeling. Many older Diaspora are resigned to their fate, and that their place of burial will be on foreign soil. They feel deeply affected by the lack of peace and stability in their birthplace. The middle and productive aged feel trapped as they are not being a part of nation-building. Their children will not return to the homeland anytime soon. The fate and emotional stability of those born during the wars in South Sudan poses an extremely complex and painful situation.

In another interesting twist, there are South Sudanese children born in East African countries. Ones such as in Uganda and

Kenya whose parents had many years with them. These children are perhaps the closest to both their parents and home. South Sudan is very near and often the parents, especially fathers, could juggle back and forth to be with their families. Most mothers stayed with the children, while the husbands were fighting inside South Sudan. Many of course died during the wars, leaving behind widows and orphans.

I was born during a relatively peaceful era of the late 1970s, which lasted until I was about seven years old.

All in all, my life has been a mixture of some early years of relative peace, then war, then relocating to the big city of Khartoum with my parents, then exile in Egypt, University in the United Kingdom, the United States of America, then neighbouring Kenya. There, I started another generation. My child was born and raised in Kenya, neighbouring South Sudan. Close but not close enough.

When my work obligated me to travel often, regionally and internationally, I too, as a single mother, became by default an absent parent. My child was raised without his father, who left us when our child was barely five months old.

This pattern of separation has continued throughout my adult life. What will be the long-term effect on 'my' son? These problems will not just 'go away'. We must find solutions!

Working with the Like-Minded

I have worked, learned from, and networked with, many like-minded progressive reformist Africans.

Most notably, I worked with:

The late Professor Wangari Mathai (RIP), on *Women Waging Peace*. It was sponsored by Noble Women Laureates and the Alternate Hunt Peace Initiative in New York. Professor Anyang Nyongo on *Building Peace Blocks in the Great Lakes Region* in 1999. A civil society joint effort where I was the South Sudan coordinator.

The late Ambassador Bethwell Kiplagat (RIP) and by proxy Professor Yash Pal Gai, on Kenya's constitutional drafting processes. A historical initiative for Kenya, which by 1999, had still been under the Lancaster drafted constitution of the 1960s (before Kenya became independent).

The formidable female lawyers in FIDA-Kenya (International Federation of Women Lawyers) regarding women's rights issues in South Sudan.

My good colleague and friend, Ms Atsango Chesoni, a human rights activist.

Former Kenya's Supreme Court Judge, Justice Dr Willy Mutunga. He worked with us during his civil society activism days in the late 1990s.

These individuals were instrumental to learn from, network with, and to influence them regarding our cause. They in turn, through their institutional organizations and active influence, were instrumental in creating awareness regarding the Sudanese conflict. This impacted both the public and the policy-makers in Kenya.

Needless to add, I worked very closely with Kenya's former Sudan Peace Talks Chief mediator, retired General Lazarus Sumbiywu. He not only successfully helped conclude Sudan's civil war, but also was a great mentor to myself.

After the signing of the peace agreement, I continued to network with these great activists. I have always focused on working with like-minded people. Ones who are extremely committed to human rights, peace, and issues forwarding the common good. In addition to them, my network began to expand, and I needed that badly for South Sudan.

In 2000 I met with an extremely active humanitarian, Ms Marit Hernaes, a former Norwegian People's Aid, NPA senior staff on South Sudan, who later on worked tirelessly on women's rights issues. She remains the chairperson of the two Sudans and Norwegian Friendship Society today. Ms Hernaes helped me significantly during my civil society work, on women's rights, and as well to remain connected with Norway during my tenure as SPLM foreign secretary 2008-2015.

In April 2009, there was a group of former European and American government senior officials who decided to hold a small think-tank group meeting in London. Its purpose centred on how to help South Sudan get through its CPA interim period. I was invited and met great individuals like a former Finnish foreign minister, a former Australian prime minister, and retired American senators and congressmen.

Former Ukrainian foreign minister Ambassador Pachovsky was there under the banner of "Step One Forum" and "Independent Diplomats" as well, former Finnish Foreign Minister Mr Johan Candelin.

This network proved extremely crucial in reaching the western world administration officials and educating them on the need that South Sudan's desire for freedom must be respected.

Both Step One Forum and Independent Diplomats representatives visited me frequently in Juba, and we communicated frequently. To any questions they asked, I was always ready to provide the answer.

It was for the good of South Sudan. I was helping to pave the way towards building its relations with the western world.

Other groups which were also instrumental in preparing us better to scientifically lobby our cause included the UK think-tank Chatham House, and South Africa's Institute for Strategic Studies, Pretoria.

These two were instrumental in scenario building. They worked at broadening the thinking and preparations for any eventuality that would lead to Sudan's final lasting peace.

South Sudan, her people, and I in particular, remain extremely grateful for the moral solidarity, technical, and logistical support of these individuals, institutions, and countries.

Their significant contributions shall always remain most appreciated. That is why I mention them here and now. I worked directly with many such groups since 1998. Truly, it has been a most fulfilling experience.

A LIFE-SAVER TOO!

Age, Gender and Colour

Political life is somewhat of an exclusive club in Africa. The most important requirements are your family name, your money. Plus, some very special skills.

They include:

- An aptitude for corruption and bullying. The ability to be cunning.
- You must have a loud mouth.
- You must be proficient regarding the ability to lie without flinching. (This is an absolute must!)
- These traits are synonymous with Africa's politicians. It is a closed club that discourages and isolates many potentially better candidates.
- To be a successful politician in Africa, one must be dirty.
- Once you are a politician or associated with politics in Africa, you will be called all sorts of names. This need not bother you.
- You have the money and power. Those that criticise you are simply meaningless noisy creatures. Ignore them.

- If you wish to be a successful African politician, you must never tell the truth about anything... ever.

At the backdrop of all this, I joined politics. My son has for years repeatedly asked me: "Why are you in politics mom? You are better than that."

This is always a question I am not able to answer straight up. The only justification I have is that there are some careers we are forced to choose, so we can make the world a better place. Yes, even if it means associating with corruption and evil.

I guess I had one of those: "Yes, I can do the impossible!" moments. For me, that moment has lasted decades.

Eighteen valuable years of my life have passed since I started walking down the road of liberation-come-peace-come-human rights activism-come-politics. Many times, I feel I have done too little; and yet other times I feel I have contributed significantly.

I still believe "Yes, I can!" Although this time, with a bit more wisdom, and the maturity of experience on my side.

I still network with like-minded individuals and groups. This is key in our African world of dirty politics. Alone, we have little hope of making even incremental changes for the betterment of the people. Even the smallest wins can give you a sense of achievement, *per se*.

The key is to adopt a non-confrontational approach. I learned that the hard way. Speaking the truth loudly and consistently to those whose consciousness are dead, will not get you anywhere. Most likely, it will make them want to commit even more wrongs.

The best approach is to work with communities and civil society groups directly. Let the people make their choices regarding demanding reforms, justice, equality, democracy, and change.

AGE, GENDER AND COLOUR

Research is also another key area that anyone who wants to survive dirty politics one must do.

By this, I mean creative research that is both formal and informal. This helps one to make the correct choice of when and where to run, and when or where to act.

Physical appearance in politics is key.

When I started out, I was young, a female, and of mixed race. It all had a major impact on me and my interactions with others.

Younger people are discouraged from starting political careers in Africa. One must be 40 years old or more, and 'connected'. This practice is equally present in liberation politics.

I am older today. Forty seems to be an acceptable age to be part of politics in Africa. However, my gender and colour will always close many doors to me. There are issues that some of us, as part of our destiny, have a duty to demystify.

We must try to make Africa accept itself, and realize its true identity. Identity is one of Africa's biggest stumbling blocks. We need to talk about and untangle this knot.

Africa's identity is not only the colours of its people, but critically, its values, culture, rich heritage, and diversity. I will not delve further into this huge topic, perhaps another book would be more apt for it.

Being fully aware of dirty politics in Africa, I joined the SPLM. Imagine that! When joining a liberation movement, one arrives with highest hopes and expectations of emancipation, justice, and equality. Here I am with liberators who are equally yearning for equality! One must assume we all share the same ideals and aspirations! That feeling didn't last for long.

Inequality should not exist in a liberation movement, or so I thought.

If you are a woman, the climb is steeper yet. You must be even older than your male counterparts before you are "allowed" in. Women must be over 50 years old generally before the 'Club' opens its doors.

These factors matter and significantly so. The younger you are, and the more female you are, the more resented, challenged and blocked you are from being a part of politics in any form.

My own experience and that of other females I worked alongside over the years are living proof of this.

That is unless you are "fortunate" enough to have encountered a top leader. That he or she must be both progressive, and dynamic enough to strategically appreciate the added value of young, up and coming, minds. Otherwise, you have little hope.

This is exactly what happened to me. I was at the right place and time when the late Dr Garang 'discovered' me. It led to many things. There was good, bad, and everything in between.

I do admit, I am extremely hard working, very focused, impressionable, persuasive, visionary, and a strategic activist. I am probably a complete 'pain' to those I see as opposing me. However, the way African politics works, I would never have had such opportunities open up to me if not for him.

On the other hand, I was resisted, challenged and forced to hurdle obstacles whenever Dr Garang was not around. I was even verbally abused to an extent to where most individuals would have quit.

That is why I developed a network and worked with likeminded activists. This helped me significantly. They made me feel that I was not alone, and always pushed me to focus on the big picture. To help save the oppressed people of Sudan.

During my days as Foreign Secretary, did the SPLM diaspora

and Sudanese political parties express shock and disbelief whenever they met me in person?

Yes, they did.

It was clearly expressed on their faces, and often in words: "We did not expect you to be a female...We did not expect you to be this young... Are you really South Sudanese?"

These were sentiments I heard far too often.

I was not "dark" enough to be South Sudanese. Being of mixed race and heritage was a major issue. Here I was, trying my best to help build people's trust and confidence in the SPLM, and my audience couldn't get past the colour of my skin! But I was not to be deterred. The big picture always guided me. The hostile attitude only made me more resilient.

When I was growing up, I began my own "colour and self-discovery" journey. I was the only light-skinned kid in the family. My South Sudanese Mother was married to a South Sudanese when she gave birth to my older siblings. She divorced him and had a brief marriage with my dad, a foreigner. I was the result. A lighter version of a typical black African kid.

I was singled out in school, church and social gatherings such as weddings, parties and funerals. In a bitterly racially divided Sudan, the 'Arab' Sudanese were favoured and dominated those of darker skin. It created great divides in all levels of our society.

I was not liked by Arabs because although I looked like them, I was a Christian. My immediate family loved me. But our extended South Sudanese family could never find it in themselves to trust or like me. I had to learn to understand and forgive them for this.

I knew that it was not their fault to hate my colour, for I symbolized their oppressors. So, I always restrained myself from reacting angrily toward any people who showed me this negative attitude. This also made me strong at a very early age.

The pain of being oppressed due to skin tone can run deeply through anyone's emotional and mental state. It was not a normal thing for the South Sudanese to hate the Arab Sudanese. It was a 'learned skill' that came about after they were maltreated, discriminated against, and marginalized.

In adulthood, I was fully aware of what was behind this stigma. I simply had to learn to accept it. But whenever I could, I would also try my best to help educate the willing. To teach that you do not judge a person by their colour. Rather, by their intentions and actions.

Some would listen, others found it too hard to understand.

I remain to this day, a singular person regarding my ideals and outlook on life. Questions about my colour will never stop. People know I belong to the nation, but I am not sure if they ever looked at me as truly one of them.

In the years after Dr Garang's death, I continued to give my all as foreign secretary. I always remained professional and a nationalist.

A significant number of African and South Sudanese politicians alike, tend to be nepotists and tribalists. Many promote and push for the ascendancy of their clan or tribe, rather than select the most competent individual.

The politics of South Sudan is rife with terrible practices. Ruling class elitism, the politics of ethnicities, incompetence, and corruption at an alarming rate. I could not identify with any of these bad governance practices. This further isolated me from my fellow 'comrades'.

My skin, gender, and my honesty meant I was increasingly

AGE, GENDER AND COLOUR

being isolated from national assignments and promotion. I worked in my post with utmost professionalism and outstanding results, but without recognition or appreciation. In fact, I was paid less than others working in roles of a similar level. No housing allowance or medical cover. Nothing.

I was determined never to let it all get the best of me! Nor should you!

Parenting

As I wrote earlier, it was during the CPA negotiations when I became pregnant with my child, Dritayi.

After he was a few months old I was back on the road being a working mom. It was not easy, but I enjoyed having a fully meaningful life of motherhood and dedicating time for peace.

The personal sacrifices were worth every bit of it.

Fortunately, my Mother was able to come and be with us for a few months while I also lucked into an amazing God-sent nanny. Her name is Lydia, and she helped me so much. I shall always be most grateful for the 11 years she dedicated to my son.

Lydia's selfless help gave me the opportunity to continue my public work. However, I always made sure I remained a loving, caring mom. He has always been my number one priority, and he inspired me to grow into a better being day after day.

Once I became a mother, all suffering children became my kids too. Real life motherhood gave me a deeper understanding into the lives of suffering children.

Their need for love, safety, a good home, and an education.

PARENTING

My dedication to human rights became even more passionate and stronger.

There is a very interesting relationship between having come from a poor family, in a war-torn country, being a victim of injustice, and the ability to fully sympathize and be extremely passionate about such issues.

I am not saying that other committed human rights activists who, for example, came from affluent families, stable societies, and generally never experienced any form of similar victimization issues, lack the ability to relate to oppressed people's issues.

In fact, to the contrary, some of the greatest human rights activists who work tirelessly and selflessly, are individuals who have never experienced any such tragedies. All the more reason to have deepest admiration and respect for such dedicated people for being committed to causes of others. This is simply noble!

My own experience, of being a "shoe-wearer", perhaps contributed centrally towards turning to activism. Obviously, impossible to prove scientifically. However, my experience becoming a mother reinforced the full-time activist in me.

Every time I held my child, I thought of a mother who is unable to do so because she is either too sick, too weak, or her child may have died from malnourishment or died as a side effect of war. Every time my child cried for milk, I felt for all those kids in the war and poverty zones who could not even get a drink of water.

This became my intertwined reality. Being a mother to my child while directly feeling the pains of the countless suffering children.

So, I could not cease my calling, or stop being a loving mom to my own child. Years passed. The hardest part of my work was whenever I had to travel. While my son was under three years old, it was possible for me to make arrangements for him. I could usually source a friend's or family's help in the destination. They would babysit my child as I attended conferences and meetings.

I encouraged and supported my son regarding the use of technology very early in his life. I ensured he owned a basic smartphone, so we would be able to email and call each other. As well, we used other social media platforms, so we could connect as often as possible.

Thankfully, from around 2004 onwards, social media and apps became increasingly available in Africa and varied. Facebook, WhatsApp, Skype, Viber etc.

We were able to communicate daily, if not hourly. I was parenting using social media to ensure that I was part of my son's life during my travels. We never missed an opportunity to connect, bond, and learn more about each other. My son grew up learning the importance of virtual media.

Both my son and I are extremely indebted and grateful to the inventors of these platforms. Indebted for our mother-child lifeline. I am simply grateful that my son was born in an era of increasingly evolving technology. Also for our ability to prioritize its usage in our relationship.

Amazingly too, even in the remotest areas of South Sudan, we could also communicate via Thuraya (satellite) phones. Albeit too expensive, it got us through the early days.

By July 2008, our ties were cut short! Independence was on the near horizon. The balance between my time for my son and my time for my country was being thrown off-kilter.

As I have written earlier, I was persuaded to become the SPLM Foreign Secretary. While I accepted conditionally upon accommodations being made for my son's best interest, it would still be difficult.

So, I found myself an affordable dwelling in Juba. I would commute back and forth, and send for my son at every opportunity!

It was, during the Interim period of the CPA, considered one of Africa's most expensive cities to live in. Especially in regard to housing costs.

The huge influx of outsiders made the number of existing dwellings totally inadequate to accommodate all the people. I managed to make myself a small haven. It was a gardenette. I tried my best to make it liveable, as well attractive, to my son. He would join me there whenever he had a school break or holidays.

During the worst of these times, I held onto him even more. At every given opportunity, I travelled to Nairobi, using my own meagre means to spend a few days with him.

A great Kenyan football legend from the 1950s, "Uncle" Joe Kadenge, was a very close family friend who helped me a greatly. My son was too young to travel on his own. Uncle Joe would escort Dritayi all the way to the plane, along with a notarized letter from myself allowing my son to travel.

The cabin crew would always take great care of my child. I would anxiously wait at the airport to receive him in Juba.

This happened frequently.

Since Uncle Joe was well known, Kenyan immigration and police authorities respected him. This helped a lot.

Both my son and I shall always and forever be grateful to him.

Fortunately, by 2008, my US-based immediate family gradually began returning to Africa. Amongst them was my brother Emmanuel Jambo, who had decided to live in Nairobi.

There he set up his life's passion, a photography business.

Uncle Emmanuel became a favourite of my son. 'Uncle' took care of him in Kenya while I was in Juba. Two years later, our youngest brother, Jambo Junior, relocated to Africa as well and chose Juba as his base.

He became my right-hand man.

We all come from the Jambo family. Our great-grandfather was a paramount chief called Jambo. The family was huge, and it was good.

Given I that was super busy with politics, and obviously taking care of my son, I did not have enough time for the rest of the extended family. I wish I could have been there for them. Jambo Jnr did all that, and much more.

As well, my soft-spoken, politically knowledgeable older brother Daniel Jambo is a great confidant. Helped me significantly to connect with street and local politics in Juba. Family indeed is always great, and will always matter.

I shall always be most grateful to all my brothers and sisters.. and my mom.

I also have extremely wonderful Kenyan friends who continuously checked on Dritayi's well-being and who remained constant in our lives to-date.

"Uncle" Julius Wako, a long-term confidant and family friend, Rose and Pauline, Ethiopian friend Helen, and Ugandan friend Yvonne. They all have been instrumental in making sure Dritayi was always taken care of when I was away for weeks and months.

The best was yet to happen. Our mother, Margaret Jambo, finally arrived back in Africa in 2010. She became a full-time grandmother to my son in Nairobi. I am forever grateful to my

PARENTING

family for being there for both my son and myself, during some of our most challenging times.

Around that time, I began contemplating quitting my foreign relations post for good. Independence was accomplished, and now we had a fully functional foreign ministry. My son needed me, and I needed a break from dirty politics. I was done! Time to move on, and work from outside politics. Perhaps we could start a peaceful, grassroots reformist movement. These were the thoughts I began turning over in my head.

If you have read this far, you know President Kiir begged me to stay on, promising reforms and a clean-up now that the country was free.

But did Mr President Kiir do it for national reasons or did he do this to survive the increasing internal power wrangles in SPLM?

Was it about reforms or about his own survival by getting rid of his rivals?

I am inclined to answer that all the SPLM ruling class, whether during armed rebellions or the government of today, are all the same.

They are betrayers of the people and their struggle for peace, freedom and equality.

It is now 2017, and I am a full-time mother to my 16-year-old son. I'm trying my utmost to compensate all the missed years.

It is introspection time regarding my career's goals and direction.

Thank you Dritayi for being a most supportive and understanding son. You taught me motherhood and parenting. Both conventional and outside the box. You were always there when I thought it was not possible to continue anymore. You were too small and young to understand many things, but you amazed me by your level of perception and wisdom. You listened to much of what I shared with you, and you always were ready with wise advice. You always loved me unconditionally and supported the bigger picture. Even if it meant at your own expense. God bless you, my boy.

Final Thoughts

The world's newest, supposedly the most sympathized with, and now the most disappointing nation; the Republic of South Sudan, increasingly became ethnically polarized.

The 2013-2014 war was said not to be about ethnicity. It was claimed by Dr Machar, the rebel leader, to be about reforms and democracy. President Kiir also reiterated the same. The war was not about Dinka against Nuer and vice versa.

So, what was it all about, really?

This is the question everyone asked. The argument that the war was about democracy did not convince me or many others.

By 2015 we were scheduled for a general election. So why start a war-making it impossible to conduct it? As citizens, we had the right to decide through ballot boxes. However, we were being robbed of that. Instead, all efforts were put into war and counter-war. As well, it generated another round of IGAD-facilitated peace process negotiations.

I spent between February 2014-May 2015 travelling on missions to Addis Ababa and Bahr Dar in Ethiopia. We "successfully" signed a peace agreement in September 2015, only for it to fall apart in a mysterious fracas in the Presidential Palace in July 2016.

Since then, South Sudan continues to suffer from mushrooming pockets of armed rebellion, an ailing economy, internal displacement, refugee status issues, hunger, diseases, and other man-made disasters.

These are all a direct negative impact of the wars. Rudderless leadership played a major part. Needless to add, the government of the north continues to sponsor armed rebellions and militias. Independence cost Bashi's government huge economic losses from the closure of access to South Sudan's teeming natural resources.

However, the President of South Sudan must shoulder a huge percentage of the blame for his failure to restore peace, order, equality, and good governance in the Country.

President Kiir is a founding president of the Republic. It is his national duty to declare general elections, and guarantee full freedom for the media, the public, and political parties. He must enable all to participate. His silence makes him a non-leader who continues to impose himself, and his corrupt incompetent government officials upon the people. His government does not seem to have any idea in what direction the Country is headed. He is a major contributor to its total collapse.

I always say to myself: I would, and could be the leader that South Sudan needs so badly. But I am a woman, barely 40, and of mixed race. South Sudan has a long way to go before accepting someone like myself. Instead, I will re-commit myself to carry on the journey I began 18 years ago.

I will fight on to ensure that South Sudan shall become the Country that so many yearned for! That so many died for! Their efforts will not be in vain!

FINAL THOUGHTS

Find a leader. One who will not abuse us! One who loves us, our country, and who we are!

20 Questions for My Son

Following are 20 questions that I posed to my son, Dritayi Jambo.

My son's journey and his feelings are immensely important to me. Dritayi had no choice regarding who his parents were, or what they were like as people. None of us does. He did, however, have a choice as to how he dealt with those things he encountered along the way.

My method was to be totally honest. I explained to him that even though some of the questions may be painful or personal, it was crucial that he participated. Other children would benefit from his experiences.

It is the hope of both of us that his answers would bring to the light a situation many children endure, but few have the opportunity to speak out about.

Dritayi willingly agreed, and we spent a good deal of time going through the questions while writing this book. His answers are frank, candid and uncensored.

20 QUESTIONS FOR MY SON

1. How old were you when you first noticed your mother was absent, and how did it feel for you?

I remember the first time that my mother went for a meeting. I was between the ages of 5 and 6. Of my exact age, I am not sure. However, I feel strongly it was around that age.

I would feel a bit sad, missing her. I thought that if I had some company, like kids my age from the neighbourhood or from school, I would feel better and less sad. However, I was alone, without company, feeling sad, and missing my Mother a lot. The way I tried to cope with this was to try to keep myself busy doing something. Activities such as playing football alone in the house compound.

Soccer has always been my favourite.

I would also play video games or watch TV.

2. Do you remember the first time your mother travelled without you? How did you feel when Mother was gone?

I was about seven years old. I remember the first time my mother went to both the USA and El Salvador. It seemed so far away from me.

She was on a work mission, and I could not accompany her. I felt our home was very empty, super quiet, and I really missed her a lot. I would again keep myself busy with my favourite activities, and kept company with my friends when possible.

One other thing I did was to enter my mother's bedroom. I could feel how empty it felt without her presence. This made me miss her even more.

3. *What did you do to cope with your mother being away? What was your routine?*

During school days, I would ensure never to miss school. I always woke up on time and went to school on time. I was always also active in school activities as football training and tournaments. These included ones outside Africa, like to Denmark, the United Kingdom, and the United States of America, in my early teens.

Prior to that, I still loved football passionately and this helped me significantly to cope with my mother's absence. I trained hard and played well. I also dutifully attended all my classes and ensured to pay attention to my studies.

I also enjoyed being with my schoolmates during class breaks. In the evenings when I returned home, I would immediately clear my homework and school assignments. I would then go outside into our courtyard and play more football with my friends in the neighbourhood.

By early evening, I went back inside, and I would have my dinner etc. Then I prepared for the next school day.

It is very important to note that I so looked forward to phone chats with my mother in the evenings. This is a bonding habit that we ensured we did every day.

We would talk on phone or text via WhatsApp on how our day had been, and just catch up with each other. These daily calls and texts brought me closer to her. It felt almost like she was there with me. I cherish and appreciate these modes of communication for bridging the distance and helping me cope with my mother's absence.

4. ***If someone asked you would you rather have your mother be at home full time, or be in a job and come home in the evenings, how would you feel?***

At my age now, I would certainly prefer my mother to have a career. It would be nice for us if she was in a job that would take her till evening hours only, so she would be back at home every day.

My reason being that I would get to be with my parent every day. I take pride knowing my mother has a career, and she is busy and able to take care of us. Wanting her to sit at home without a job would be selfish of me. It's healthy that my mother has her own career to pursue.

5. ***Did you like your mother travelling alone back when you were around 3 years old?***

Definitely not! At 3 I always wanted my mother to be with me. But I also tremendously enjoyed travelling with her then. However, I never liked her travelling alone when I was younger. It was always painful for me to cope with her absence.

6. ***How lonely did you feel when your mother travelled?***

I felt very lonely. I am an only child, and I had to do my best to figure things out by myself. I tried always to be around good friends my age and to also be busy with both school and sports. Also, I tried my best to make sure my phone was charged so I could communicate with my mother every day while she was away. In my own experience, I do not appreciate my mother having travelled alone on work missions when I was younger.

Over the years, I simply learnt to cope with this absence. We also tried to reach out to each other often. This helped a lot. I am not sure how other kids could have coped. But I know it was never easy for me.

Kids need to be surrounded by good family, friends, school, and activities such as sports. They need to be always communicating with their parents. I know this will help kids a lot, as it has helped me significantly.

7. Were you ever mistreated when your mother was away on travels?

Never! Fortunately, I have been a very lucky kid to have had good people around me. My mother has extremely strong public relations and management skills.

She always ensured to provide for us a good home in a peaceful neighbourhood. We had wonderful neighbours and an excellent school where the teachers all took good care of me.

As well, she employed an excellent nanny, "Auntie Lydia". She took super good care of me for eleven years. Generally, I have always appreciated all these wonderful people around me. My mother respected them highly and treated them well. She always told me that when you treat people well, they reciprocate in the same way. So, I maintained politeness and good manners in both school, and at home.

The fortunate thing as well, was my mother tried to never travel for long periods consecutively. She always tried her best to be with me at least after one week or ten days. Rarely was she away for more than that. Often too, she tried her best to arrange for me to accompany her when she could, and when it was permitted.

8. How was school for you?

School has always been both enjoyable socially, and as a learning experience for me. I always participated in my class activities and in all sports passionately, especially football. I missed my mother during parent's meetings, or when I needed her to sign my daily school homework book, or when there were other school activities needing her presence.

My mother tried her best to commute from Juba, South Sudan where she was based at her work, to Nairobi, Kenya, where I stayed due to school.

9. How was school for you, especially your school friends, when your mother was away on work travels?

I always enjoyed my school and having great school friends. It kept us busy with a unique style of education combined with personal growth values, and of course great sports such as football.

However, I still vividly remember some painful memories of how other kids and my school friends were picked up from school by their parents. I was not! Often, I wished and yearned so much that my mother could be like the other kids' parents, and be the one to pick me up from school. This is something I still remember.

When mother was around, she jokingly used to call herself "my chauffeur". I was thrilled and thoroughly enjoyed those drives with her whenever she dropped and picked me up from school. We would have a lot of great chats, laughs, and catch up time.

These were also the moments when my mother talked heart to heart with me about many things. It was also when I told her a lot about my school work challenges. I often promised her to be always a better student and kid.

We would both watch the greenery and the beautiful scenes and trees in Nairobi.

The Jacaranda tree I remember my mother being particularly very fond of. She loves all nature generally. These shall always remain as beautiful bonding memories with my mother.

10. How did home feel like when your mother was away?
Although my mother and I worked so hard to ensure an extremely cozy home, with all basic things and wonderful people around us; our home felt empty when she was gone.

I would come from school and immediately I would notice my mother's voice not there. Room after room, including her bedroom all, seemed silent. That was always a tough experience for me, especially when I was younger. Even the food did not taste the same. I always loved my mother's cooking and eating with her. But when she was away, I ate alone. I simply had to learn to cope, and I always looked forward to our evening phone or texts chats. For once, I would feel like she was at home with me.

11. Do you hate politics of South Sudan because of your mother being away from you when you were small? How do you feel about the failures in your country? The economy, hunger, refugees, and wars etc.
I do not like politics generally because I have seen first hand how politics and politicians mess up a lot of things. You would think they are the children.

I take it a little more personally. Politics often took my mother away from me when I was young. At some time when I was around 11-13 years old, I began to appreciate my mother's, and my own, sacrifices for South Sudan. Especially when I saw her work contributed toward our freedom and peace in 2011. I tried my best to support my mother then by often joining her in Juba, during my school holidays.

Those were moments I truly cherished. I was with my mother and I was in our free independent country. But honestly, as time went by, once again just like when I was younger, I began disliking politics again from 2013 onwards.

During that time, there were a lot of political confusion and wars. I often feared for her life. I was also mad at those military and political people who caused

so much pain to all South Sudanese, including my mother's own hard effort to bring peace to my country.

I felt like she had wasted many years of her life for a country that seemed to have no appreciation for peace and a good way of living.

Seriously, a lot did not make any sense to me from 13 up to now.

What country, politicians, and armed forces can destroy their own country like that? All those people suffering from hunger and diseases. I truly despise politics.

On the social level, because I am a child who was born during the war and grew up outside my country, I honestly feel more at home in Kenya. That is where I was born and raised.

This makes me feel extremely sad.

How I wish once our country gained its independence, it could have focused on making a home for its people. Instead, the so-called 'powers that be' focused on corruption and wars.

So now, at sixteen, I am still living outside my country. I have no beautiful memories of my original home.

I pray one day there shall be peace, justice, and development.

I want to be able to visit more often and learn about my people and our culture more in-depth.

My wonderful mother always tries her best to teach me about all that. But I wish to live it in real life in a peaceful, friendly, and loving environment.

I noticed sometimes how rude military and police mistreat people around the streets in Juba, this discourages me a lot, very sadly.

12. How did you keep yourself busy when your mother was away?
I developed the mental attitude that I simply must keep myself busy. I went to school without absence. I thoroughly enjoyed it, even during school holidays and when she was away. I am a sociable, outgoing, extroverted person.

I have very good friends with whom I interacted with easily and without complications. I also love sports (especially football), and athletics.

Football remains my number one sport. As I played and trained over the years, I also developed an increasingly keen interest in learning about football professionally. I voraciously followed the various African and International leagues and teams. I studied the different ways they play football. I follow it passionately still.

Other things I occupied myself with (especially as I grew older), include knowing about animals, geography, the world affairs, computers, and cooking.

13. Was it good that you had nice neighbours including two kids near your age?
As an only child, I consider myself extremely lucky that for over 10 years (since I was about ten months old) we had very good

next door neighbours. Being close to my age, they became like brother and sister to me.

We lived side by side for ten years, and we celebrated Christmas, New Year's, and our birthdays together. We went to our school events together and went to playgrounds in our earlier years accompanied by our parents. They kept me company when my mother was away on work missions. This always helped me cope with missing her. I shall always cherish those moments with my two childhood friends.

14. How is it being an only child?

Being a child alone without brothers or sisters is not nice. I always wished I could have had other siblings like many other families. Having them is like having more company and friends, and always together. What a wonderful feeling that would be.

When my mother went away on work travels are the times I missed and wished and wished I had a brother, or a sister, or both. Anything! If I had, I would not have felt as lonely and alone.

For example, at Christmas time my mother would often be home with me.

But if I had siblings, I am sure our Christmas would have been nicer by far. Also, at dinnertime or when watching a movie at home, it would have been so great with a group of us!

Even at times like going out for play or games, I think it would have been more fun if I had a brother or a sister to be with me. Basically, being a lone child is not an experience I enjoyed. I will always wish it wasn't just me.

15. Did your mother's work inspire you? And why?
I admire my mother's determination and strength.

Unfortunately, I wish my mother chose another type of work than politics. I fully admire her commitment to human rights and for desiring a better world for the underprivileged and poor people. But at what cost was it to us both?

I watch my mother and listen to her speaking about humanity and making the world a better place. I have always admired her passion and resilience despite all the challenges.

She never gives up. She is the most determined person I know.

Her work, determination, and strength inspire me greatly. It gives me a feeling of happiness whenever she is helping others, such as the homeless, orphans, and poor people.

Very importantly, seeing my mother working with rigid, egoistic, primitive, retarded, and seemingly infinitely stupid people, makes me admire her resilience. I feel very inspired as a young person to see a woman like her survive in such hostile working environment.

It inspires me greatly that my mother is this warm, patient, and determined person. She goes so far to achieve peace, human rights, respect, and justice. She would almost go to any length bravely to rescue innocent victims. My mother remains my role model.

16. Did you mother's work ever make you feel insecure or afraid for her security?
Honestly, I never felt bad about her. Nor did I feel insecure about myself.

However, I was always on my toes, and praying for my mother's safety.

This all started in December 2013 when rebels tried to overthrow the Government in Juba, and my mother was there during heavy fighting.

There were days when we could not even communicate. There was no telephone, internet, or flights to and from Juba.

She was caught up there, and I simply could not sleep, as I was very worried regarding her safety. Due to the nature of her political work, I have learnt over the years that vocal human rights activists, and genuine politicians who stand for reforms (like my mother), had deadly political enemies.

As a result, often her neighbourhood in Juba would be raided by unidentifiable armed personnel at night. They would attack anyone on sight. This scared me a lot regarding her security. I felt quite justified in advising her that she needed not to live in Juba where her life was always at risk.

17. How do you feel being raised by a single mother? Do you wish you had both parents?

I always wished and hoped that I had both parents. For a mom and dad like many other children. I do miss having a dad in my life since birth almost. Being raised by my mother alone, however, made me feel very loved by her. Also by her strength and ability to fully take care of me.

My mother and I are like friends. We have no barriers, and she raised me with values and principles. She used modern methods of bringing me up. I always felt free to be myself and to express my dreams, aspirations, and goals in life.

Sometimes I wonder, if I had both parents, would my dad and mom have given me the same quality upbringing? I also see other children who have both parents, where one parent or both are abusive or too harsh.

That really sits badly with me.

With my mother, she always respected my decisions. For example, when I graduated from kindergarten to primary school, she asked me (I was about 5 years old) whether I wanted to continue in the same school. I answered in the affirmative. She asked me the same question when I completed primary school and would begin secondary. Again, I answered affirmatively.

My mother always respected my space. Be it my bedroom, or with my friends, or my activities. She always preferred not to over-interfere with, or disturb me. As well, she always tried her best to encourage and support my passion for sport and football. One thing I also appreciate about my mother is how proud she has always been of me and my achievements. Our home has always had all my medals and school merits certificates beautifully framed in the house. She always told me as well how proud and loving is she toward me.

18. Do you ever blame your mother's work for her status as a single mom?

I think in a way, maybe her over-occupation, and (maybe) too much passion for human rights and peace work, especially on South Sudan, may have played some negative role in my mother not enjoying a normal social life. Maybe this could be a factor in her remaining a single parent to this day.

I really do not know fully because I am only sixteen years old. I am just guessing. I wish my mother could have a conventional, ordinary life so she can socialize and interact more with people, other than politicians and activists. Life has more to offer! There are so many varieties of hobbies and activities which I wish she would do.

19. Do you ever blame your dad for being a single parent's kid?
At times I wonder why my dad left us. Yes, in a way I blame him.

He left us when I was 5 months old, so I really do not know his reasons for leaving.

My mother has tried her best to make me forgive him for having left me. I try my best as well not to get too consumed by this huge gap in my life. I am also extremely fortunate that I have uncles (my mother's brothers) who have always been part of my life since I was small. My uncles Daniel, Emmanuel Jambo, and Jambo Jr. are great to me.

This has been instrumental in my life.

As well, my mother's good friend "uncle" Julius Wako has been very constant and consistent in my life since I was 4 years old. Often, he and I watched football together and we support the same team.

Remaining positive and focused while being surrounded by loving caring people, especially my strong mother, who has always been very capable of being both "mom and dad", helped me significantly not to dwell on negativity of my father's absence in my life. However, ideally and like any other kid, especially boys, I always wish my father was in my life. I have fully forgiven him, and one day we shall meet and shall talk.

20. What are your ideals, values and aspirations for yourself and this world?
My ideals include being a good citizen of the world. A productive innovative person in some great field/career. My values include equality of gender, race, and age. To me, I do not like to see either a five-year-old or a fifty-year-old being mistreated. Human beings regardless of age, gender, or race, are all the same and must be

treated equally and fairly. My aspirations always vary, and I am quite a dynamic sort of "well-rounded" teenager. I am attracted to technology, sports (especially football) and fascinated by how things are made and developed. As well, I love international culture, news, and human-related activities.

Specifically, my aspirations are narrowed around technology, financial empowerment and innovation. I definitely wish to be happy, whether it be helping people around me, or globally.

I want to do some things that I personally like. I am a person who is increasingly evolving around my desire to be a well-balanced person.

I want to focus on taking care of personal issues/life and giving back to the world.

Critically, I admire, and I am equally inspired by, my mother's resilience, determination and passion. I would most definitely take a lot of this from her. I will try to personalize it to my own context, and would-be lifestyle in the future, in a way that I choose.

Thank you.

Cairo Egypt September 1999 during an official SPLM visit Suzanne Jambo accompanied Dr. John Garang. Looking on Ms. Regina Osman Ms. Muna Khojiali.

With South Sudanese President Kiir Juba October 2013.

During an all Sudanese human rights conference, Suzanne Jambo and activists, Kampala Uganda 2000.

Dritayi Jambo and his mother Susan Jambo.

www.ingramcontent.com/pod-product-compliance
Lightning Source LLC
Chambersburg PA
CBHW020651300426
44112CB00007B/334